GALLSTONE DIET COOKBOOK FOR NEWLY DIAGNOSED

Recipes for Natural Gallbladder Treatment and Digestive Promotion

Mary J. Barnes RDN

ACKNOWLEDGMENT

This cookbook wouldn't have been possible without the unwavering support of my family and friends, who patiently taste-tested countless recipes and offered invaluable feedback. Your encouragement fueled my passion for creating delicious, healing meals.

I am deeply grateful to the medical professionals and researchers who have dedicated their lives to understanding gallstones and digestive health. Your knowledge and insights have been instrumental in shaping this cookbook.

A special thanks to my editor, Maris F, Clark Ph.D. whose expertise and guidance helped refine this cookbook into its final form. Your diligent attention to detail and unwavering belief in this project are appreciated.

To the newly diagnosed individuals who inspired this cookbook, I hope these recipes bring you comfort, nourishment, and a renewed sense of cooking joy. May this cookbook be a valuable resource on your journey toward optimal health.

WHY THIS COOKBOOK?

Let's be real. A gallstone diagnosis can feel like a life sentence of bland, boring food. But it doesn't have to be. This isn't your average diet cookbook filled with complicated recipes and hard-to-find ingredients.

This cookbook is your ticket to delicious, easy-to-make meals that support your gallbladder and promote healthy digestion. It's packed with real-world advice and simple swaps that make sticking to a gallstone diet feel effortless.

Here's what sets this cookbook apart:

- **Flavor-First:** We believe healthy food should never be boring. You'll find vibrant, flavorful recipes that you'll enjoy eating.

- **Simplicity:** We get it, you're busy. That's why our recipes use simple ingredients and straightforward instructions.

- **Real-World Advice:** We've been there. This book is full of practical tips and tricks for making a gallstone diet work for your life.

- **Support System:** You're not alone. This cookbook is a friendly guide on your journey to better gallbladder health.

Whether you're a kitchen pro or a newbie, this book will give you the tools and confidence to take control of your health, one delicious meal at a time.

TABLE OF CONTENTS

HOW TO MAKE THIS COOKBOOK WORK FOR YOU

1. Start with the Basics:

The first few chapters explain what gallstones are and how they affect your body. This information helps you grasp why this diet is important.

2. Find Your Perfect Plan:

We've included a simple meal plan to get you started. You can follow it as is or use it as inspiration to create your plan.

3. Explore the Recipes:

The heart of this book is the recipes. Each one is carefully chosen to be gentle on your gallbladder while still being tasty and satisfying.

- **Breakfasts** to kickstart your day
- **Lunches** that are easy to pack or make at home
- **Dinners** for the whole family
- **Snacks and Desserts** for those in-between moments

4. Make it Yours:

Feel free to swap ingredients, adjust portions, or try different combinations. As you get more comfortable, you'll find what works best for you.

5. Tips and Tricks:

Throughout the book, you'll find helpful tips on cooking methods, shopping for ingredients, and managing your diet when eating out.

INTRODUCTION

GALLSTONE DIET FOR NEWLY DIAGNOSED

As a sudden pain shot through my side, I became suddenly nauseous with the realization that this was just another gallstone attack. I could no longer ignore the fact that I was suffering anymore, it wasn't just about how to manage the pain but also how to take charge of my health. Amidst my hazy discomfort, one simple phrase bubbled up: "Food is medicine." But where was the cookbook that would guide me on this new cooking journey?

I felt lost and overwhelmed by my gallstone diagnosis, as probably did you. Advice from the physician—low-fat, high-fiber diet— sounded straightforward enough; however, making this delicious in real life seemed insurmountable. My usual go-to recipes were off-limits and I felt besieged by confusing dietary restrictions all around me. There was an urge in me for a mentor or companion to help me navigate through these unexplored lands.

Therefore, powered by both frustration and determination, I embarked on a mission to create a cookbook that only existed in my mind. As such, I read numerous medical journals and took advice from nutritionists not to leave out uncountable experiments in my kitchen. Along the way were other people who had similar experiences of fear and panic as mine. Their tales were relatable to me, thus reinforcing the need for a cookbook that not only had recipes but also provided support and encouragement. That journey is chronicled in this book – it was a tough journey for me, and I have taken all those challenges into my heart and soul. It is more than a recipe collection; it's a lifeline toward living a healthier and happier life after a diagnosis of gallstones. Whether you are new to cooking or an old hand at it, whether you live alone or have a family to feed, this is your book.

These cookbooks abound in mouthwatering dishes with uncomplicated directions that cater to various preferences. We'll begin with the rudiments, unraveling the mysteries of gallstone diets as well as explaining fats, fibers, quantities, and portions. You'll understand how to fill up your cupboards with key things and make good choices while eating out. This cookbook is something beyond mere instructions; rather it celebrates taste: It shows that healthy eating can be interesting and fun in some kind of way. You'll be able to make a variety of different meals such as tasty soups and stews, colorful salads, and fulfilling main dishes which will provide essential substances for your body and make you feel satisfied.

There are stories about my life, and some tips that I got during the process while writing this book. My favorite low-fat cooking skills, my replacements for high-fat ingredients, or my ways to gourmet simple food will be revealed to you. I also want you to meet others who share their winning experience over the Gallstone diet, including some amazing culinary adventures.

This cookbook is your "better health" good friend whether it's your first gallstone diagnosis or not. It's a well of inspiration, handy stuff, and comforting knowledge that you're not alone.

So, roll up your sleeves, grab your apron, and let's get cooking!

The Benefits of a Gallstone Diet

1. **Reduces Gallstone Formation:**

- **Low in Cholesterol:** Gallstones are often formed due to excess cholesterol in bile. By limiting high-cholesterol foods (like fatty meats, fried foods, and full-fat dairy), you can decrease the risk of new stones forming.
- **High in Fiber:** Fiber-rich foods (fruits, vegetables, whole grains) help regulate cholesterol levels and promote healthy bowel movements, reducing the chance of gallstone development.

2. **Manages Symptoms:**

- **Low in Fat:** Fatty foods can trigger gallbladder contractions, leading to pain and discomfort. A low-fat diet can help prevent these attacks.
- **Avoids Trigger Foods:** Certain foods, like greasy or spicy dishes, can aggravate gallstone symptoms.

3. **Improves Digestion:**

- **High in Fiber:** Fiber promotes regular bowel movements and prevents constipation, which can exacerbate gallstone issues.

- **Includes Probiotics:** Fermented foods (yogurt, sauerkraut) contain beneficial bacteria that aid digestion and may even help dissolve cholesterol gallstones.

4. **Boosts Energy Levels:**

- **Nutrient-Dense:** A gallstone diet focuses on whole, unprocessed foods packed with vitamins, minerals, and antioxidants, providing sustained energy throughout the day.

- **Eliminates Sugar Crashes:** Cutting back on sugary drinks and processed snacks helps stabilize blood sugar levels, preventing energy dips and promoting overall vitality.

5. **Promotes Weight Loss:**

- **Lower in Calories:** A healthy gallstone diet naturally reduces calorie intake, leading to gradual, sustainable weight loss.

- **Improves Metabolism:** Eating regular meals and choosing nutrient-dense foods can help boost your metabolism and support weight management efforts.

CHAPTER 1:
GALLSTONES AND YOUR DIET

Did you know that nearly one in four women and one in twelve men will develop gallstones during their lifetime? It's a surprisingly common condition, yet many people don't realize how their dietary choices can influence gallstone formation.

Your gallbladder, a small sac located beneath your liver, stores and releases bile, a digestive fluid that breaks down fats. When bile composition becomes unbalanced, gallstones, hardened deposits ranging from tiny grains to golf balls, can form.

While gallstones may not always cause symptoms, when they do, they can be quite uncomfortable. *Sharp pain in the upper right abdomen, radiating to the back or shoulder blade, is a common complaint. This pain, known as biliary colic, often occurs after eating fatty foods. Other symptoms include nausea, vomiting, indigestion, and bloating.*

The good news is that you can take control of your gallbladder health and reduce your risk of gallstones through dietary changes. By understanding the science behind gallstones and making informed food choices, you can promote a healthy balance in your gallbladder

and prevent these troublesome stones from forming. Cholesterol and bilirubin are the primary culprits behind gallstone formation. Cholesterol is a type of fat found in certain foods, while bilirubin is a waste product produced when your body breaks down red blood cells. When these substances become too concentrated in bile, they can crystallize and form gallstones.

A gallstone-friendly diet focuses on reducing cholesterol intake and promoting a healthy balance of nutrients. This means opting for lean proteins like poultry, fish, beans, and lentils instead of fatty red meats. It also involves incorporating plenty of fiber-rich foods, such as fruits, vegetables, and whole grains. Fiber helps bind cholesterol in your digestive system, preventing it from being absorbed into your bloodstream.

A low-fat diet is also crucial for managing gallstones. Fatty foods, especially fried foods, fatty meats, and full-fat dairy products, can trigger gallbladder contractions and lead to painful attacks. Limiting your fat intake can minimize the risk of these uncomfortable episodes.

In addition to what you should limit, there are also foods you should actively incorporate into your diet. Fruits and vegetables, with their high water and fiber content, help dilute bile and prevent it from becoming too concentrated. Whole grains, like brown rice, quinoa, and oats, provide sustained energy and support healthy digestion. Certain spices and herbs, such as turmeric, ginger, and dandelion root, have also been shown to have beneficial effects on gallbladder health. They can help reduce inflammation, promote bile flow, and even support the breakdown of existing gallstones.

Remember, a gallstone diet isn't just about what you eat—it's also about how you eat. Eating smaller, more frequent meals can help prevent your gallbladder from becoming overloaded. Staying hydrated by drinking plenty of water throughout the day is also important for maintaining healthy bile flow.

It's important to note that everyone's dietary needs are different, and it's always best to consult with your doctor or a registered dietitian to develop a personalized plan. They can help you identify your specific triggers and create a diet that aligns with your individual health goals.

If you've been recently diagnosed with gallstones, don't despair. By embracing a gallstonc-fricndly dict, you can take charge of your health and enjoy a life filled with flavorful, nourishing meals. This cookbook is your guide to that journey, providing you with delicious recipes and practical tips to support your gallbladder health every step of the way.

Types of Gallstones

Cholesterol stones, as the name suggests, are primarily made of cholesterol, a type of fat found in your blood. These are the most common types of gallstones, accounting for roughly 80% of cases.

Pigment stones, on the other hand, are made of bilirubin, a substance formed when your body breaks down red blood cells. These stones are less common but can still cause significant discomfort.

Recognizing the Warning Signs: Symptoms of Gallstones

Gallstones often lurk silently within your gallbladder, causing no noticeable symptoms. However, when they do act up, they can make their presence known in a variety of ways. The most common symptom is a sharp, intense pain in your upper right abdomen, often radiating to your back or shoulder blade. This pain, known as biliary colic, typically occurs after a fatty meal and can last for several hours.

Other telltale signs of gallstones include:

- Nausea and vomiting

- Indigestion and heartburn

- Bloating and gas

- Changes in bowel habits, such as light-colored stools or diarrhea

If you experience any of the symptoms mentioned above, it's crucial to seek medical attention promptly. Early diagnosis and treatment can prevent complications and improve your quality of life. Your doctor can perform various tests, such as an ultrasound or CT scan, to confirm the presence of gallstones and determine the best course of treatment.

Risk Factors for Gallstones

While anyone can develop gallstones, certain factors increase your risk. Understanding these risk factors can help you make informed choices about your lifestyle and diet to minimize your chances of developing these pesky stones.

- **Age:** Your risk of gallstones increases as you get older, especially after the age of 40.

- **Gender:** Women are more prone to gallstones than men, possibly due to hormonal fluctuations.

- **Weight:** Being overweight or obese significantly increases your risk, as excess body fat can disrupt the balance of cholesterol in bile.

- **Diet:** A diet high in saturated fats, cholesterol, and refined carbohydrates can contribute to gallstone formation. Conversely, a diet rich in fiber and healthy fats can help protect your gallbladder.

- **Genetics:** If you have a family history of gallstones, you may be genetically predisposed to developing them.

Taking Charge of Your Gallbladder Health

A silver lining to this is that your gallbladder health can be influenced by what you eat. A diet friendly to gallstones will prevent the formation of new stones, alleviate symptoms in those with already existing ones, and promote general digestion well-being.

This cookery book is aimed at supporting you throughout this journey providing you with yummy healthy recipes customized to meet your specific requirements. More about the principles of a gallstone diet in the next section will highlight some foods that should be embraced and others that should be avoided.

Self-Reflection Questions:

1. What are my current dietary habits, and how might they be impacting my gallbladder health?

_____

_____

_____

_____

2. Am I aware of the potential risk factors for gallstones in my own life?

_____

_____

_____

_____

3. What are my triggers for gallbladder discomfort?

_____

_____

_____

4. How can I make sustainable changes to my diet to promote gallbladder health?

_____

_____

_____

_____

_____

5. What resources (cookbooks, nutritionists, etc.) can I utilize to support my dietary journey?

_____

_____

_____

_____

_____

CHAPTER 2:
GALLSTONE-FRIENDLY GROCERY LIST

Fruits & Vegetables:

High-Fiber Fruits:

Apples

Berries (Strawberries, Blueberries, Raspberries)

Pears

Oranges

Grapefruits

High-Fiber Vegetables:

Broccoli

Brussels Sprouts

Carrots

Leafy Greens (Kale, Spinach, Romaine)

Squash

Sweet Potatoes

Other Healthy Choices:

Avocados

Cucumbers

Tomatoes

Peppers

Mushrooms

Whole Grains:

Breads & Cereals:

Whole-Wheat Bread

Brown Rice

Quinoa

Oats

Barley

Whole-Wheat Pasta

Other Options:

Whole-Wheat Crackers

Popcorn (Air-Popped)

Brown Rice Cakes

Lean Protein:

Poultry:

Skinless Chicken or Turkey Breast

Ground Chicken or Turkey (Lean)

Fish:

Salmon

Tuna

Cod

Trout

Sardines

Legumes:

Lentils

Chickpeas

Black Beans

Kidney Beans

Other Options:

Tofu

Tempeh

Eggs (In Moderation)

Healthy Fats:

Nuts & Seeds:

Almonds

Walnuts

Cashews

Sunflower Seeds

Chia Seeds (In Moderation)

Oils:

Olive Oil and Avocado Oil

Avocado: Enjoy in moderation

Low-Fat Dairy (Optional):

Milk:

Skim Milk

Almond Milk

Soy Milk

Yogurt: Low-fat or nonfat plain yogurt

Cheese:

Low-Fat Cottage Cheese

Part-Skim Mozzarella

Low-Fat Greek Yogurt

Herbs & Spices:

Flavor Enhancers:

Turmeric

Ginger

Garlic

Onion

Basil

Oregano

Rosemary

Thyme

Others:

Cinnamon

Cumin

Coriander

Black Pepper

Additional Items:

Broth: Low-Sodium Vegetable Or Chicken Broth

Vinegar: Apple Cider Vinegar, Balsamic Vinegar

Lemon & Lime Juice: Freshly squeezed for flavor and acidity

Foods to Limit or Avoid:

- **Fried Foods:** French fries, chips, and fried chicken are notorious for packing a double punch of unhealthy fats and cholesterol, putting your gallbladder in overdrive.

- **Fatty Meats:** Red meat, bacon, sausage, and hot dogs can be high in saturated fats that contribute to gallstone formation. Choose lean protein sources instead for a happier gallbladder.

- **Full-Fat Dairy:** Whole milk, full-fat cheese, and ice cream might be tempting, but their high-fat content can trigger gallbladder contractions and leave you in pain. Opt for low-fat or non-fat dairy options for a healthier alternative.

- **Refined Grains:** White bread, white rice, and sugary cereals lack the fiber your gallbladder needs to function smoothly. Switch to whole grains for better digestion and a lower risk of gallstones.

- **Sugary Drinks:** Soda, sweetened tea, and energy drinks are not only loaded with empty calories but can also contribute to weight gain, a major risk factor for gallstones. Choose water or unsweetened beverages to keep your gallbladder happy.

Embrace a Healthier Path:

- **Read Food Labels:** Become a savvy shopper by checking food labels for fat, sugar, and fiber content. Make informed choices to prioritize your gallbladder health.

- **Choose Fresh:** Fresh fruits and vegetables are packed with fiber, vitamins, and minerals that support gallbladder function. Ditch processed options and embrace the vibrant flavors of nature.

- **Cook at Home:** Take charge of your diet by cooking at home. This allows you to control the ingredients and cooking methods, ensuring healthier meals that nourish your gallbladder.

- **Variety is Key:** Don't limit yourself to a few foods. Aim for a colorful plate filled with a variety of fruits, vegetables, whole grains, and lean proteins to get all the nutrients you need.

- **Listen to Your Body:** Your body is your best guide. Pay attention to how different foods affect you and adjust your diet accordingly. If a particular food triggers discomfort, it's best to avoid it.

CHAPTER 3:

BREAKFAST RECIPES FOR GALLBLADDER HEALTH

1. Scrambled Tofu with Vegetables

This recipe is a fantastic alternative to scrambled eggs, offering a plant-based, low-fat, and cholesterol-free option that's perfect for the gallstone diet. The tofu provides protein, while the vegetables add fiber and essential nutrients.

INGREDIENTS:

- 1 block firm or extra-firm tofu, crumbled
- 1 tablespoon olive oil
- 1/2 cup chopped onion
- 1/2 cup chopped bell pepper (any color)
- 1/2 cup chopped mushrooms
- 1/4 cup chopped spinach
- 1/4 teaspoon turmeric
- 1/4 teaspoon black pepper
- Salt to taste
- Optional: chopped fresh herbs (parsley, chives) for garnish

COOKING INSTRUCTIONS:

1. Heat olive oil in a non-stick pan over medium heat.

2. Add onion, bell pepper, and mushrooms. Sauté until softened, about 5 minutes.

3. Add crumbled tofu and turmeric. Cook, stirring frequently, until tofu is heated through, about 5 minutes.

4. Stir in spinach and cook until wilted about 1 minute.

5. Season with black pepper and salt to taste.

6. Garnish with fresh herbs if desired.

COOKING TECHNIQUES:

- This quick cooking method helps retain the nutrients in the vegetables and adds flavor to the tofu.

- Crumbling the tofu creates a texture similar to scrambled eggs.

NUTRITIONAL VALUES PER SERVING (APPROXIMATE):

- Calories: 150

- Protein: 15g

- Fat: 8g

- Carbohydrates: 5g

- Fiber: 2g

Serving Portion: This recipe makes about 2 servings.

Cooking Time: 15 minutes

Prep Time: 10 minutes

DIET RECIPE NOTE:

This dish is completely compatible with the gallstone diet. It is low in fat, cholesterol-free, and full of fiber-rich veggies. Tofu is a fantastic source of plant-based protein, while turmeric provides anti-inflammatory benefits. This meal is highly modifiable; for diversity, try adding zucchini, broccoli, or carrots.

2. Oatmeal with Almond Milk and Berries

A comforting and nutritious breakfast, oatmeal with almond milk and berries is a perfect choice for a gallstone-friendly diet. It's packed with fiber from oats and berries, low in fat, and naturally sweet, making it a delicious and healthy way to start your day.

INGREDIENTS:

- 1/2 cup rolled oats
- 1 cup unsweetened almond milk
- 1/2 cup mixed berries (strawberries, blueberries, raspberries)
- 1 tablespoon chopped nuts (almonds, walnuts)
- 1/4 teaspoon ground cinnamon (optional)
- 1 teaspoon honey or maple syrup (optional, for sweetness)

COOKING INSTRUCTIONS:

1. In a small saucepan, combine oats and almond milk.
2. Bring to a boil, then reduce heat and simmer for 5-7 minutes, or until oats are cooked through and the mixture thickens.
3. Remove from heat and stir in berries, nuts, and cinnamon (if using).
4. Sweeten with honey or maple syrup if desired.
5. Serve warm.

COOKING TECHNIQUES:

- This gentle cooking method allows the oats to absorb the almond milk and become creamy.
- Stirring occasionally prevents the oats from sticking to the bottom of the pan.

NUTRITIONAL VALUES PER SERVING (APPROXIMATE):

- Calories: 250
- Fat: 5g
- Carbohydrates: 40g
- Fiber: 7g
- Protein: 8g

Serving Portion: 1 bowl

Cooking Time: 10 minutes

Prep Time: 5 minutes

DIET RECIPE NOTE:

This meal is great for the gallstone diet since it is low in fat, high in fiber, and has no processed grains or added sweets. Almond milk is an excellent dairy-free option for individuals who are lactose intolerant or wish to limit their dairy consumption. The berries give antioxidants and fiber, while the almonds contribute healthful fats and protein.

ADDITIONAL TIPS:

- You can use steel-cut oats instead of rolled oats for a heartier texture. Just adjust the cooking time accordingly.

- Feel free to experiment with different types of berries and nuts to find your favorite combination.

- For added flavor, you can stir in a pinch of nutmeg or ginger along with the cinnamon.

_____

_____

_____

_____

_____

_____

_____

_____

_____

_____

3. Greek Yogurt Parfait

A delightful and nutritious breakfast or snack option, Greek yogurt parfait is packed with protein, fiber, and probiotics, making it an excellent choice for a gallstone-friendly diet. It's also incredibly versatile, allowing for an endless selection of different fruits, nuts, and seeds.

INGREDIENTS:

- 1 cup plain non-fat Greek yogurt
- 1/2 cup mixed berries (strawberries, blueberries, raspberries)
- 1/4 cup granola (low-fat, no added sugar)
- 1 tablespoon chia seeds (optional)
- 1 teaspoon honey or maple syrup (optional, for added sweetness)

COOKING INSTRUCTIONS (ASSEMBLY):

1. In a glass or jar, layer half of the Greek yogurt at the bottom.
2. Top with half of the mixed berries.
3. Sprinkle half of the granola and chia seeds (if using) over the berries.
4. Repeat layers with the remaining yogurt, berries, granola, and chia seeds.
5. Sprinkle with honey or maple syrup if desired.

COOKING TECHNIQUES:

- Layering: The key to a visually appealing parfait is to layer the ingredients evenly.
- Mixing: If preferred, you can mix the yogurt, berries, and granola instead of layering.

NUTRITIONAL VALUES PER SERVING (APPROXIMATE):

- Calories: 250
- Protein: 18g
- Fat: 5g
- Carbohydrates: 30g
- Fiber: 6g
- Sugar: 12g (mostly from fruit)

Serving Portion: 1 parfait

Cooking Time: 5 minutes (assembly only)

Prep Time: 5 minutes (washing and cutting fruit)

This Greek yogurt parfait is ideal for a gallstone diet since it is low in fat, high in fiber, and contains no processed sugars. To maintain gallbladder health, use a low-fat, unsweetened granola. You may control the sweetness by adding or removing the honey or maple syrup. To increase the nutritional content, sprinkle with nuts or seeds such as almonds or pumpkin seeds for beneficial fats and fiber.

_____

_____

_____

_____

_____

_____

_____

_____

_____

_____

_____

4. Gallstone-Friendly Quinoa Breakfast Bowl

Kickstart your day with a hearty and nutritious quinoa breakfast bowl that's gentle on your gallbladder. This recipe is packed with fiber, protein, and essential nutrients to support your overall health and healthy living.

INGREDIENTS:

- 1/2 cup uncooked quinoa
- 1 cup low-fat milk (almond, soy, or skim milk)
- 1/2 teaspoon vanilla extract
- A pinch of cinnamon or nutmeg (optional)
- Toppings: fresh berries, chopped nuts, seeds, a drizzle of honey (optional)

COOKING INSTRUCTIONS:

1. Rinse the quinoa thoroughly under cold water.

2. In a saucepan, combine the quinoa, milk, vanilla extract, and spices (if using).

3. Bring to a boil, then reduce heat to low, cover, and simmer for 15-20 minutes, or until the quinoa is cooked and the liquid is absorbed.

4. Remove from heat and let stand for 5 minutes.

5. Fluff the quinoa with a fork and divide it into bowls.

6. Top with your favorite fresh berries, chopped nuts, seeds, and a drizzle of honey (if desired).

COOKING TECHNIQUES:

- Cooking the quinoa over low heat allows it to absorb the liquid slowly and become fluffy.
- Fluffing the quinoa with a fork helps to separate the grains and prevent them from clumping together.

NUTRITIONAL VALUES PER SERVING (APPROXIMATE):

- Calories: 250
- Protein: 8g
- Fiber: 5g
- Fat: 5g
- Carbohydrates: 35g

Serving Portion: This recipe makes one serving.

Cooking Time: 20-25 minutes

Prep Time: 5 minutes

This quinoa breakfast dish is ideal for a gallstone-friendly diet. It is low in fat and high in fiber, with no processed grains or added sugars. The toppings may be adjusted to your preferences and dietary requirements. For example, if you're managing your sugar eating, you might substitute unsweetened almond milk for dairy milk or leave out the honey entirely.

_____

_____

_____

_____

_____

_____

_____

_____

_____

_____

5. Gallstone-Friendly Sweet Potato Hash

This sweet potato hash is a delicious and nutritious dish that aligns perfectly with a gallstone-friendly diet. It's packed with fiber-rich vegetables, lean protein, and healthy fats, making it a satisfying and nourishing meal option.

INGREDIENTS:

- 2 medium sweet potatoes, diced
- 1 tablespoon olive oil
- 1/2 onion, diced
- 1 bell pepper (any color), diced
- 1/2 cup chopped mushrooms
- 1/2 cup cooked lean ground turkey or chicken (optional)
- 1 teaspoon smoked paprika
- 1/2 teaspoon cumin
- 1/4 teaspoon salt
- 1/4 teaspoon black pepper
- Fresh herbs for garnish (parsley, cilantro, etc.)

COOKING INSTRUCTIONS:

1. Heat the olive oil in a large pan over medium heat.

2. Add the diced sweet potatoes and cook for 5-7 minutes, or until slightly softened.

3. Add the diced onion, bell pepper, and mushrooms to the pan. Cook for another 5 minutes, or until the vegetables are tender.

4. If using ground turkey or chicken, add it to the pan and cook until browned.

5. Season with smoked paprika, cumin, salt, and pepper. Stir well to combine.

6. Cook for an additional 2-3 minutes, or until the flavors meld together.

7. Garnish with fresh herbs before serving.

COOKING TECHNIQUES:

- This technique is used to cook vegetables and ground meat in a small amount of oil, promoting even browning and flavor development.

- The addition of spices like smoked paprika and cumin helps the flavor of the dish without adding unnecessary fat or sodium.

NUTRITIONAL VALUES PER SERVING (APPROXIMATE):

- Calories: 250

- Protein: 10g

- Fat: 12g

- Carbohydrates: 25g

- Fiber: 5g

Serving Portion: This recipe yields approximately 4 servings.

Cooking Time: 20-25 minutes

Prep Time: 10-15 minutes

DIET RECIPE NOTE:

This sweet potato hash is appropriate for a gallstone diet since it excludes fried meals, fatty meats, full-fat dairy, refined cereals, and sweet drinks. It is high in fiber, vitamins, and minerals, making it a nutritious and delicious meal option for those with gallstones. This meal may be modified by adding other gallstone-friendly veggies such as zucchini or spinach, or by substituting a different lean protein source such as beans or lentils.

_____

_____

_____

_____

_____

_____

_____

_____

6. Vegetable Omelet

A light and healthy breakfast or lunch option, the vegetable omelet is a perfect fit for the Gallstone diet. It's low in fat, packed with nutrients, and easy to customize with your favorite vegetables.

INGREDIENTS:

- 2 large eggs
- 1/4 cup chopped vegetables (bell peppers, onions, mushrooms, spinach, tomatoes, etc.)
- 1 tablespoon milk (optional, use low-fat or non-fat)
- Salt and pepper to taste
- 1 teaspoon olive oil

COOKING INSTRUCTIONS:

1. Mix the eggs and milk (if using) in a bowl. Season with salt and pepper.

2. Heat the olive oil in a non-stick pan over medium heat.

3. Add the chopped vegetables and sauté until softened, about 3-5 minutes.

4. Pour the egg mixture over the vegetables.

5. As the edges of the omelet set, gently lift them with a spatula, allowing the uncooked egg to flow underneath.

6. Once the omelet is mostly set but still slightly runny on top, fold it in half.

7. Cook for another minute or two until the omelet is cooked through.

8. Slide the omelet onto a plate and serve.

COOKING TECHNIQUES:

- Quickly cooking the vegetables in a small amount of oil helps to retain their nutrients and flavor.
- Thoroughly mixing the eggs and milk incorporates air, creating a light and fluffy omelet.
- Carefully folding the omelet prevents it from breaking and ensures even cooking.

NUTRITIONAL VALUES (PER SERVING):

- Calories: Approximately 150
- Protein: 12g
- Fat: 9g
- Carbohydrates: 3g
- Fiber: 2g

Serving Portion: 1 omelet

Cooking Time: 10 minutes

Prep Time: 5 minutes

This veggie omelet is suitable for the gallstone diet since it excludes fried meals, fatty meats, and full-fat dairy. It contains nutritious veggies and may be adjusted to your preferences. If you are sensitive to fats, you can remove the milk and use cooking spray for olive oil.

_____

_____

_____

_____

_____

_____

_____

_____

_____

_____

7. Sautéed Greens with Poached Egg

This dish is a delicious and nutritious way to enjoy leafy greens, packed with fiber and nutrients that are beneficial for gallbladder health. The poached egg adds protein and richness, while the sautéed greens provide a vibrant base.

INGREDIENTS:

- 1 tablespoon olive oil
- 2 cloves garlic, minced
- 4 cups mixed greens (such as kale, spinach, or Swiss chard), chopped
- Salt and pepper to taste
- 2 large eggs
- 1 tablespoon white vinegar (optional, for poaching eggs)

COOKING INSTRUCTIONS:

1. Heat the olive oil in a large pan over medium heat.

2. Add the minced garlic and cook for about 30 seconds, until fragrant.

3. Add the chopped greens to the pan and sauté until wilted, about 3-5 minutes. Season with salt and pepper to taste.

4. While the greens are cooking, fill a separate saucepan with about 3 inches of water. Add the vinegar (if using) and bring to a cooking.

5. Crack one egg into a small bowl. Gently slide the egg into the simmering water. Repeat with the second egg.

6. Poach the eggs for about 3-4 minutes, or until the whites are set and the yolks are still runny.

7. Remove the eggs with a slotted spoon and drain on a paper towel-lined plate.

8. Divide the sautéed greens between two plates and top each with a poached egg.

9. Season the eggs with additional salt and pepper, if desired.

COOKING TECHNIQUES:

- This quick cooking method helps preserve the nutrients in the greens while adding flavor.
- This gentle cooking method results in tender, perfectly cooked eggs.

NUTRITIONAL VALUES PER SERVING (APPROXIMATE):

- Calories: 250
- Protein: 14g

- Fat: 17g

- Carbohydrates: 8g

- Fiber: 4g

Serving Portion: This recipe makes two servings.

Cooking Time: 15-20 minutes.

Prep Time: 5-10 minutes.

DIET RECIPE NOTE:

This meal is appropriate for the Gallstone diet because it contains healthy fats from olive oil, fiber-rich veggies, and lean protein from eggs. It avoids fried meals, fatty meats, high-fat dairy, refined grains, and sweet drinks. You can vary the amount of olive oil used depending on your dietary requirements.

_____

_____

_____

_____

_____

_____

_____

_____

_____

_____

8. Avocado Toast with Smoked Salmon

This recipe is a perfect blend of healthy fats, protein, and fiber, making it a great choice for a gallstone-friendly breakfast or snack. Avocado provides heart-healthy fats, smoked salmon is a good source of protein, and whole-grain bread adds fiber to aid digestion.

INGREDIENTS:

- 1 ripe avocado
- 1 tablespoon lemon juice
- Salt and pepper to taste
- 2 slices of whole-grain bread, toasted
- 4 ounces smoked salmon
- Optional toppings: red onion slices, capers, dill, everything bagel seasoning

COOKING INSTRUCTIONS:

1. Mash the avocado with a fork in a small bowl.
2. Add lemon juice, salt, and pepper, and mix well.
3. Spread the avocado mixture evenly on the toasted bread.
4. Top with smoked salmon and any desired toppings.

COOKING TECHNIQUES:

- Toasting the bread adds a bit of crunch and prevents the toast from getting soggy.
- Mashing the avocado with a fork creates a chunky texture, but you can use a food processor for a smoother thickness.
- Adding lemon juice to the avocado helps prevent it from browning.

NUTRITIONAL VALUES PER SERVING (APPROXIMATE):

- Calories: 350
- Fat: 20g
- Protein: 15g
- Carbohydrates: 20g
- Fiber: 8g

Serving Portion: 2 slices of toast

Cooking Time: 5 minutes

Prep Time: 5 minutes

This meal is great for the gallstone diet since it excludes all of the things that should be limited or avoided. It is low in saturated fat, cholesterol, and processed carbs, yet high in fiber and beneficial fats.

TIPS FOR MODIFYING FOR GALLBLADDER HEALTH:

- **Limit the number of smoked salmon:** While smoked salmon is a healthy protein source, it is high in sodium. If you are sensitive to sodium, use a smaller number of smoked salmon or choose a low-sodium variety.

- **Add more vegetables:** For an extra boost of fiber and nutrients, add sliced cucumbers, tomatoes, or sprouts to your toast.

- **Use whole-grain bread:** Choose a whole-grain bread that is high in fiber and low in sugar.

- **Choose low-fat toppings:** If you are concerned about fat intake, use a light cream cheese or cottage cheese instead of the avocado.

_____

_____

_____

_____

_____

_____

_____

_____

_____

9. Spinach and Mushroom Frittata

This Spinach and Mushroom Frittata is a delicious and nutritious breakfast or brunch option for those following a gallstone diet. It's packed with fiber-rich vegetables, lean protein from egg whites, and healthy fats. The cooking method, baking, avoids the use of excessive oil, making it a gallbladder-friendly choice.

INGREDIENTS:

- 6 large egg whites
- 1 cup chopped fresh spinach
- 1/2 cup sliced mushrooms
- 1/4 cup chopped onion
- 1/4 cup shredded low-fat cheddar cheese (optional)
- 1 tablespoon olive oil
- Salt and pepper to taste

COOKING INSTRUCTIONS:

1. Heat oven to 350°F (175°C).
2. In a large bowl, mix egg whites, salt, and pepper.
3. Heat olive oil in an oven-safe pan over medium heat. Add onion and cook until softened.
4. Add mushrooms and cook until they release their moisture.
5. Stir in spinach and cook until wilted.
6. Pour the egg white mixture over the vegetables in the pan.
7. Sprinkle with cheese, if desired.
8. Transfer the pan to the oven and bake for 15-20 minutes, or until the frittata is set and lightly browned.

COOKING TECHNIQUES:

- Used to soften the onions and mushrooms.
- The primary cooking method, which helps the frittata set and brown evenly.

NUTRITIONAL VALUES PER SERVING (1/4 OF FRITTATA):

- Calories: approximately 100
- Protein: 12 grams
- Fat: 4 grams

- Carbohydrates: 3 grams

- Fiber: 2 grams

Serving Portion: This recipe yields 4 servings.

Prep time: 10 minutes

Cooking time: 20 minutes

This frittata is ideal for a gallstone diet since it prevents fried meals, fatty meats, and full-fat dairy. The use of egg whites lowers cholesterol levels, while the addition of spinach and mushrooms provides important fiber. If you are sensitive to fats, omit the cheese or use a reduced quantity.

TIPS:

- Feel free to experiment with different vegetables like bell peppers, zucchini, or broccoli.

- Add herbs and spices like thyme, basil, or garlic powder for extra flavor.

- Serve with a side salad for a complete and satisfying meal.

_____

_____

_____

_____

_____

_____

_____

_____

_____

10. Chia Seed Pudding

Chia seed pudding is a nutritious and delicious breakfast or snack option that perfectly aligns with a gallstone-friendly diet. It's riches with fiber, protein, and healthy fats, making it a satisfying and filling choice that won't irritate your gallbladder.

INGREDIENTS:

- 1/4 cup chia seeds
- 1 cup unsweetened almond milk (or other low-fat milk alternative)
- 1 tablespoon maple syrup (optional, or use a sugar substitute)
- 1/2 teaspoon vanilla extract
- Pinch of cinnamon (optional)
- Toppings: fresh berries, sliced bananas, chopped nuts

COOKING INSTRUCTIONS:

1. In a jar or bowl, combine chia seeds, almond milk, maple syrup (if using), vanilla extract, and cinnamon.

2. Stir well to ensure the chia seeds are evenly distributed.

3. Cover and refrigerate for at least 2 hours, or preferably overnight, to allow the chia seeds to absorb the liquid and create a pudding-like thickness.

4. Before serving, give the pudding a good stir to break up any clumps.

5. Top with your favorite fruits, nuts, or a mixture of additional maple syrup, if desired.

PREP TECHNIQUES:

- Simply mix the ingredients and let the refrigerator do the work.
- If you prefer a smoother texture, you can blend the mixture for a few seconds before refrigerating.

NUTRITIONAL VALUES (PER SERVING):

- Calories: approximately 150
- Protein: 5 grams
- Fiber: 11 grams
- Fat: 7 grams (mostly healthy fats from chia seeds)
- Sugar: varies depending on the sweetener used

Serving Portion: One serving is approximately 1/2 cup.

Cooking Time: But requires refrigeration for at least 2 hours.

Prep Time: 5 minutes

DIET RECIPE NOTE:

This chia seed pudding dish is ideal for a gallstone-friendly diet. It's low in fat, high in fiber, and has no cholesterol or processed sugars. Chia seeds contain omega-3 fatty acids, which can help lower inflammation and promote gallbladder health. Feel free to experiment with different toppings to add diversity and taste to your pudding while adhering to your diet plan.

11. Smashed Chickpea Salad Wrap

This Smashed Chickpea Salad Wrap is a delicious and nutritious meal option that is perfect for those following a gallstone-friendly diet. It is riches with fiber, protein, and healthy fats, making it a satisfying and fulfilling meal. The wrap is also very versatile and can be easily selected to your liking.

INGREDIENTS:

- 1 can (15 ounces) chickpeas, drained and rinsed
- 1/2 avocado, mashed
- 2 tablespoons plain Greek yogurt (non-fat or low-fat)
- 1 tablespoon lemon juice
- 1/4 teaspoon garlic powder
- 1/4 teaspoon onion powder
- Salt and pepper to taste
- 4 large whole wheat tortillas
- Optional toppings: lettuce, tomato, cucumber, sprouts

COOKING INSTRUCTIONS:

1. In a medium bowl, mash the chickpeas with a fork until they are mostly broken down but still have some texture.

2. Add the mashed avocado, Greek yogurt, lemon juice, garlic powder, onion powder, salt, and pepper to the bowl. Stir until well mixed.

3. Spread the chickpea salad evenly over the tortillas.

4. Top with your desired toppings.

5. Roll up the tortillas and enjoy!

COOKING TECHNIQUES:

- The chickpeas are mashed with a fork to create a chunky texture.
- The ingredients are mixed in a bowl.
- The chickpea salad is spread evenly over the tortillas.
- The tortillas are rolled up to create wraps.

NUTRITIONAL VALUES PER SERVING:

- Calories: 250

- Protein: 10g

- Fat: 12g

- Carbohydrates: 28g

- Fiber: 8g

Serving Portion: This recipe makes 4 servings.

Cooking Time: 10 minutes

Prep Time: 10 minutes

DIET RECIPE NOTE:

This dish is suited for the gallstone diet. It's low in fat, cholesterol, and sugar, but high in fiber. Chickpeas are high in protein and fiber, while avocados contain healthful fats. Greek yogurt gives smoothness and protein, while lemon juice provides flavor and acidity. Whole wheat tortillas are rich in fiber.

_____

_____

_____

_____

_____

_____

_____

_____

_____

_____

12. Sweet Potato Hash Browns

A delicious and healthy alternative to traditional hash browns, this recipe swaps out white potatoes for nutrient-rich sweet potatoes. Baked instead of fried, these hash browns are low in fat and cholesterol, making them a great addition to a gallstone-friendly diet.

INGREDIENTS:

- 2 medium sweet potatoes, peeled and grated
- 1 tablespoon olive oil
- 1/2 teaspoon salt
- 1/4 teaspoon black pepper
- Optional: 1/4 teaspoon garlic powder or other spices for flavor

COOKING INSTRUCTIONS:

1. Heat oven to 400°F (200°C).

2. In a large bowl, combine grated sweet potatoes, olive oil, salt, pepper, and any additional spices.

3. Line a baking sheet with parchment paper.

4. Divide sweet potato mixture into equal portions and form into patties.

5. Place patties on a prepared baking sheet and bake for 20-25 minutes, flipping halfway through, until golden brown and crispy.

COOKING TECHNIQUES:

- Use a box grater or food processor to shred the sweet potatoes.
- Baking instead of frying reduces fat content and promotes a crispy texture.
- Flipping the patties halfway through ensures even browning.

NUTRITIONAL VALUES PER SERVING (1 PATTY):

- Calories: 100-120
- Fat: 2-3g
- Cholesterol: 0mg
- Carbohydrates: 20-25g
- Fiber: 3-4g
- Protein: 2-3g

Serving Portion: 1-2 patties per serving

Cooking Time: 20-25 minutes

Prep Time: 10 minutes

DIET RECIPE NOTE:

This dish is suitable for the Gallstone diet since it excludes fried meals, fatty meats, full-fat dairy, refined cereals, and sweet drinks. It is high in fiber and vitamins, and the baking procedure makes it a better option than regular fried hash browns.

ADDITIONAL TIPS:

- For extra flavor, add chopped herbs like parsley or cilantro to the sweet potato mixture.

- Serve with a dollop of plain Greek yogurt or a poached egg for a complete breakfast.

- Enjoy these hash browns as a side dish with grilled chicken or fish for a healthy and satisfying meal.

13. Quinoa Breakfast Burrito

This quinoa breakfast burrito is a delicious and nutritious way to start your day. It's riches with protein, fiber, and healthy fats, making it a satisfying and energizing meal. Plus, it's easy to specify with your favorite fillings, so you can make it your own.

INGREDIENTS:

- 1 cup cooked quinoa
- 1/4 cup black beans, rinsed and drained
- 1/4 cup corn, fresh or frozen
- 1/4 cup chopped red onion
- 1/4 cup chopped bell pepper (any color)
- 1/4 cup chopped tomatoes
- 1/4 cup salsa
- 1/4 cup shredded low-fat cheese
- 2 whole-wheat tortillas
- Optional: avocado slices, hot sauce

COOKING INSTRUCTIONS:

1. In a large bowl, combine the cooked quinoa, black beans, corn, red onion, bell pepper, tomatoes, salsa, and cheese.
2. Warm the tortillas in a dry pan or microwave.
3. Divide the quinoa mixture evenly between the tortillas.
4. Fold the tortillas up like burritos.
5. Enjoy immediately or wrap and store in the refrigerator for later.

COOKING TECHNIQUES:

- Sautéing: You can sauté the vegetables in a small amount of olive oil for added flavor.
- Grilling: For a crispy texture, grill the burritos for a few minutes on each side.

NUTRITIONAL VALUES PER SERVING (1 BURRITO):

- Calories: 350
- Protein: 15g
- Fat: 12g
- Carbohydrates: 45g

- Fiber: 10g

Serving Portion: 1 burrito

Cooking Time: 10 minutes

Prep Time: 10 minutes

DIET RECIPE NOTE:

This meal is appropriate for the Gallstone diet since it is low in fat, and high in fiber, and does not include fried foods, fatty meats, full-fat dairy, refined cereals, or sweetened drinks. It's an excellent way to add quinoa into your morning routine and receive a healthy dose of protein and fiber to begin the day.

To further adapt this recipe to the gallstone diet:

- Use low-sodium black beans and salsa.

- Omit the cheese or use a low-fat or dairy-free option.

- Add additional vegetables like spinach or mushrooms for extra fiber and nutrients.

_____

_____

_____

_____

_____

_____

_____

_____

14. Salmon and Vegetable Quiche

This Salmon and Vegetable Quiche is a delicious and healthy meal option that is suitable for a gallstone diet. It is riches in nutrients and low in fat, making it a great choice for those looking to manage their gallbladder health.

INGREDIENTS:

- 1 (9-inch) unbaked pie crust (choose a whole-wheat or gluten-free option)
- 1 cup cooked salmon, flaked
- 1 cup chopped broccoli florets
- 1/2 cup chopped carrots
- 1/4 cup chopped onion
- 3 large eggs
- 1 cup low-fat milk
- 1/2 cup shredded cheddar cheese (optional)
- Salt and pepper to taste

COOKING INSTRUCTIONS:

1. Heat oven to 375°F (190°C).
2. In a large bowl, combine the flaked salmon, broccoli, carrots, and onion.
3. In a separate bowl, mix the eggs, milk, cheese (if using), salt, and pepper.
4. Pour the egg mixture over the vegetables and salmon.
5. Pour the mixture into the pie crust.
6. Bake for 45-50 minutes, or until the quiche is golden brown and set.
7. Let cool for a few minutes before slicing and serving.

COOKING TECHNIQUES:

- The quiche is baked in the oven to set the custard and cook the vegetables.
- The eggs and milk are mixed to create a smooth custard.
- The vegetables are chopped into small pieces to ensure even cooking.

NUTRITIONAL VALUES PER SERVING:

- Calories: 250
- Fat: 12g

- Cholesterol: 150mg

- Sodium: 300mg

- Carbohydrates: 15g

- Protein: 18g

Serving Portion: 1 slice

Cooking Time: 45-50 minutes

Prep Time: 15 minutes

DIET RECIPE NOTE:

This meal is ideal for a gallstone diet since it is low in fat and cholesterol. It is also rich in protein and fiber. The veggies include necessary vitamins and minerals, while the salmon is rich in omega-3 fatty acids. To make this dish even healthier, substitute a whole-wheat or gluten-free pie crust. You may also leave out the cheese to lower the fat level.

_____

_____

_____

_____

_____

_____

_____

_____

_____

_____

15. Green Smoothie Bowl

This great and refreshing Green Smoothie Bowl is riches in nutrients and fiber, making it a great choice for a gallstone-friendly breakfast or snack. It's a delicious way to incorporate leafy greens, fruits, and healthy fats into your diet while supporting your gallbladder health.

INGREDIENTS:

- 1 cup spinach or kale
- 1/2 frozen banana
- 1/2 cup frozen berries (strawberries, blueberries, raspberries)
- 1/4 avocado
- 1/2 cup unsweetened almond milk or coconut milk
- 1 tablespoon chia seeds or ground flaxseeds (optional)
- Toppings: Sliced fruit, berries, granola, nuts, seeds

COOKING INSTRUCTIONS:

1. Combine all ingredients in a blender and blend until smooth and creamy. Add more milk if needed to reach the desired consistency.

2. Pour into a bowl and top with your favorite toppings.

3. Enjoy immediately!

COOKING TECHNIQUES:

- Blending: The key technique is blending all the ingredients until smooth.
- Freezing Ingredients: Freezing the banana and berries helps create a thicker, creamier texture.

NUTRITIONAL VALUES PER SERVING (APPROXIMATE):

- Calories: 250-300 kcal
- Protein: 5-7 g
- Fat: 10-15 g
- Carbohydrates: 30-35 g
- Fiber: 8-10 g

Serving Portion: This recipe makes one generous serving.

Cooking Time: 5 minutes

Prep Time: 5 minutes

This Green Smoothie Bowl is ideal for a gallstone diet since it's low in fat, high in fiber, and full of minerals. It avoids all of the items that should be limited or avoided on a gallstone diet. However, be wary of the toppings you select. Choose fresh fruits, berries, nuts, and seeds over sweet granola or high-fat toppings such as coconut flakes.

Additional Tips:

- Feel free to experiment with different greens and fruits based on your preferences and what's in season.

- Add a scoop of protein powder for an extra boost if desired.

- If you prefer a sweeter smoothie, add a drizzle of honey or maple syrup.

- For added creaminess, you can add a spoonful of plain Greek yogurt or a few tablespoons of silken tofu.

Self-Reflection Questions:

1. What are my typical breakfast choices, and do they align with a gallstone-friendly diet?

_____

_____

_____

_____

_____

_____

2. Am I willing to explore new breakfast options to support my gallbladder health?

_____

_____

_____

3. What are my personal preferences for breakfast flavors and textures?

4. How can I make time for a nutritious breakfast even on busy mornings?

5. What challenges do I anticipate in making sustainable changes to my breakfast routine?

CHAPTER 4:

LUNCH GALLBLADDER DIET

1. Grilled Chicken Salad

This light and refreshing Grilled Chicken Salad is a perfect lunch or dinner option for those following a gallstone diet. It's riches in lean protein, fiber, and nutrients while avoiding high-fat ingredients that can trigger gallbladder issues.

INGREDIENTS:

- 1 boneless, skinless chicken breast (about 4 ounces)
- 1 tablespoon olive oil
- 1/4 teaspoon salt
- 1/4 teaspoon black pepper
- 4 cups mixed greens (spinach, romaine, arugula, etc.)
- 1/2 cup chopped vegetables (cucumber, bell peppers, carrots, etc.)
- 1/4 cup chopped nuts or seeds (walnuts, almonds, pumpkin seeds, etc.)
- 2 tablespoons light vinaigrette dressing (balsamic, lemon, or herb vinaigrette)

INSTRUCTIONS:

1. Heat the grill to medium heat.
2. Rub chicken breast with olive oil, salt, and pepper.
3. Grill chicken for 5-7 minutes per side, or until cooked through.
4. Remove chicken from the grill and let rest for 5 minutes before slicing.
5. In a large bowl, combine mixed greens, chopped vegetables, nuts, and sliced chicken.
6. Sprinkle with vinaigrette dressing and toss to coat.
7. Serve immediately.

COOKING TECHNIQUES:

- Grilling the chicken adds flavor and keeps it lean.
- Chop the vegetables and nuts to your desired size.
- Toss the salad gently to combine all ingredients and coat them with dressing.

NUTRITIONAL VALUES PER SERVING (APPROXIMATE):

- Calories: 300-350 kcal

- Protein: 25-30 g

- Fat: 15-20 g

- Carbohydrates: 10-15 g

- Fiber: 5-7 g

Serving Portion: This recipe makes one generous serving.

Cooking Time: 15-20 minutes

Prep Time: 10 minutes

DIET RECIPE NOTE:

This Grilled Chicken Salad is great for the gallstone diet since it is low in fat, high in protein and fiber, and does not include fried meals, fatty meats, full-fat dairy, or sugary drinks. It's a tasty and healthy method to promote gallbladder health.

Tips:

- Marinate the chicken in herbs and spices for extra flavor.

- Use a different of colorful vegetables for added nutrients and visual appeal.

- Experiment with different types of nuts and seeds for added texture and flavor.

- If you like a creamier dressing, you can use a light vinaigrette made with Greek yogurt or avocado.

2. Turkey Lettuce Wraps

These delicious Turkey Lettuce Wraps are a great lunch or light dinner option for those following a gallstone diet. They are rich in lean protein, fiber, and fresh vegetables, making them a nutritious and satisfying meal. The absence of fried components, fatty meats, and refined grains makes it an ideal choice for individuals managing gallbladder health.

INGREDIENTS:

- 1 pound ground turkey
- 1 tablespoon olive oil
- 1 onion, chopped
- 2 cloves garlic, minced
- 1 red bell pepper, chopped
- 1/2 cup chopped water chestnuts
- 1/4 cup hoisin sauce
- 2 tablespoons soy sauce (low sodium)
- 1 tablespoon rice vinegar
- 1 teaspoon sesame oil
- 1/4 teaspoon ground ginger
- Pinch of red pepper flakes
- Salt and pepper to taste
- Butter lettuce leaves

COOKING INSTRUCTIONS:

1. Heat olive oil in a large pan over medium heat.

2. Add ground turkey and cook until browned, breaking it up into crumbles.

3. Add onion, garlic, and bell pepper. Cook until softened.

4. Stir in water chestnuts, hoisin sauce, soy sauce, rice vinegar, sesame oil, ginger, and red pepper flakes.

5. Cooking for 5 minutes, or until heated through.

6. Season with salt and pepper to taste.

7. Spoon the turkey mixture into butter lettuce leaves and serve.

- The main cooking technique used is sautéing, which involves cooking the ingredients in a small amount of oil over medium heat.

- The sauce is cooked to allow the flavors to meld.

NUTRITIONAL VALUES PER SERVING (APPROXIMATE):

- Calories: 250 kcal

- Protein: 25 g

- Fat: 12 g

- Carbohydrates: 10 g

- Fiber: 2 g

Serving Portion: This recipe yields approximately 4 servings.

Cooking Time: 20 minutes

Prep Time: 10 minutes

DIET RECIPE NOTE:

These turkey lettuce wraps are ideal for a gallstone diet since they are low in fat and cholesterol, high in protein, and filled with fiber-rich veggies. They also include plenty of vitamins and minerals. To further lower fat content, use ground turkey breast instead of ordinary ground turkey.

_____

_____

_____

_____

_____

3. Salmon and Quinoa Bowl

This Salmon and Quinoa Bowl is a powerhouse of delicious nutrition, perfectly great for those newly diagnosed with gallstones or looking to support their gallbladder health. Riches with lean protein, healthy fats, fiber, and essential nutrients, this dish is a delicious and satisfying way to nourish your body while keeping your gallbladder happy.

INGREDIENTS:

- 1 salmon fillet (4-6 ounces), skinless and boneless
- 1 cup cooked quinoa
- 1 cup mixed greens (spinach, arugula, kale)
- 1/2 cup roasted vegetables (broccoli, carrots, zucchini)
- 1/4 avocado, sliced
- 2 tablespoons lemon vinaigrette dressing (olive oil, lemon juice, Dijon mustard, herbs)
- Salt and pepper to taste

INSTRUCTIONS:

1. Heat oven to 400°F (200°C).
2. Season the salmon fillet with salt and pepper.
3. Bake the salmon for 12-15 minutes, or until cooked through and flaky.
4. While the salmon is baking, prepare the quinoa according to package instructions.
5. In a bowl, combine the cooked quinoa, mixed greens, roasted vegetables, and sliced avocado.
6. Top with the baked salmon fillet.
7. Sprinkle with lemon vinaigrette dressing.
8. Season with salt and pepper to taste.

COOKING TECHNIQUES:

- The salmon is baked in the oven for a healthy cooking method.
- Vegetables are roasted to help their flavor and tenderness.
- The bowl is assembled with cooked quinoa, greens, roasted vegetables, salmon, avocado, and dressing.

NUTRITIONAL VALUES PER SERVING (APPROXIMATE):

- Calories: 450-500 kcal
- Protein: 30-35 g
- Fat: 20-25 g (mostly healthy unsaturated fats from salmon and avocado)

- Carbohydrates: 30-35 g

- Fiber: 10-12 g

Serving Portion: This recipe makes one generous serving.

Cooking Time: 20-25 minutes

Prep Time: 10 minutes

DIET RECIPE NOTE:

This Salmon and Quinoa Bowl goes nicely with a gallstone diet. It excludes fried meals, fatty meats, and full-fat dairy while adding lean protein (salmon), fiber-rich quinoa and veggies, and healthy fats (avocado). The lemon vinaigrette dressing adds taste without using excessive fats or sugars. It's a nutritious and enjoyable meal that promotes gallbladder health.

4. Lentil Soup

This hearty and delicious Lentil Soup is a comforting and nutritious option for those following a gallstone diet. Riches with fiber, protein, and essential nutrients, lentils are a great alternative to fatty meats, and this soup is easy to digest and gentle on the gallbladder.

INGREDIENTS:

- 1 cup brown or green lentils, rinsed and drained
- 4 cups low-sodium vegetable broth
- 1 tablespoon olive oil
- 1 onion, chopped
- 2 carrots, chopped
- 2 celery stalks, chopped
- 2 cloves garlic, minced
- 1 teaspoon dried thyme
- 1/2 teaspoon cumin
- Salt and pepper to taste
- Fresh parsley, chopped (optional, for garnish)

COOKING INSTRUCTIONS:

1. Heat the olive oil in a large pot over medium heat. Add the onion, carrots, and celery and cook until softened, about 5 minutes.

2. Add the garlic, thyme, and cumin and cook for another minute until aroma.

3. Stir in the lentils and vegetable broth. Bring to a boil, then reduce heat to low, cover, and cook for 20-25 minutes, or until lentils are tender.

4. Season with salt and pepper to taste.

5. Serve warm, garnished with fresh parsley if desired.

COOKING TECHNIQUES:

- Sautéing the vegetables in olive oil adds flavor and helps them soften.
- Simmering the lentils in broth allows them to cook through and absorb flavor.

NUTRITIONAL VALUES PER SERVING (APPROXIMATE):

- Calories: 230 kcal
- Protein: 18 g

- Fat: 4 g

- Carbohydrates: 35 g

- Fiber: 15 g

Serving Portion: This recipe makes 4 servings.

Cooking Time: 30 minutes

Prep Time: 15 minutes

DIET RECIPE NOTE:

This lentil soup is ideal for a gallstone diet since it is low in fat, high in fiber, and cholesterol-free. It avoids all of the items that should be limited or avoided on a gallstone diet. You may vary the dish by adding chopped spinach, kale, or zucchini. A dash of red pepper flakes or a splash of lemon juice can provide more flavor.

_____

_____

_____

_____

_____

_____

_____

_____

5. Quinoa Stuffed Bell Peppers

A a delicious and nutritious meal rich in flavor and fiber, Quinoa Stuffed Bell Peppers are a great addition to your gallstone-friendly diet. They provide a satisfying combination of complex carbohydrates, protein, and vegetables while avoiding trigger foods for gallbladder issues.

INGREDIENTS:

- 2 bell peppers (any color)

- 1/2 cup quinoa, cooked

- 1/2 cup black beans, rinsed and drained

- 1/2 cup corn, frozen or fresh

- 1/4 cup chopped onion

- 1/4 cup chopped red pepper

- 1/4 cup chopped tomatoes

- 1 tablespoon olive oil

- 1/2 teaspoon chili powder

- 1/4 teaspoon cumin

- 1/4 teaspoon garlic powder

- Salt and pepper to taste

COOKING INSTRUCTIONS:

1. Heat oven to 375°F (190°C).

2. Cut the bell peppers in half lengthwise and remove the seeds and membranes.

3. In a large bowl, combine cooked quinoa, black beans, corn, onion, red pepper, tomatoes, olive oil, chili powder, cumin, garlic powder, salt, and pepper. Mix well.

4. Fill each bell pepper half with the quinoa mixture.

5. Place the stuffed peppers in a baking bowl and bake for 25-30 minutes, or until the peppers are tender and the filling is heated through.

COOKING TECHNIQUES:

- Sauté the vegetables in olive oil to help their flavor and soften them slightly before mixing them with the quinoa.

- Baking the stuffed peppers allows the flavors to meld together and the peppers to become tender.

- Calories: 250-300 kcal

- Protein: 10-12 g

- Fat: 5-7 g

- Carbohydrates: 35-40 g

- Fiber: 10-12 g

Serving Portion: This recipe makes two servings (one bell pepper half per serving).

Cooking Time: 25-30 minutes

Prep Time: 15 minutes

DIET RECIPE NOTE:

This Quinoa Stuffed Bell Peppers dish is great for the Gallstone diet since it eliminates fried meals, fatty meats, full-fat dairy, refined grains, and sweetened drinks. It's high in fiber, lean protein, and complex carbs, making it a healthful and delicious lunch for individuals concerned about their gallbladder.

To further adapt the recipe:

- Use brown rice or another whole grain instead of quinoa.

- Add other vegetables like zucchini, mushrooms, or spinach.

- Use a low-sodium or no-salt-added canned tomato product.

- Top with fresh herbs like cilantro or parsley for added flavor and antioxidants.

6. Wraps with Lettuce and Tuna Salad

These refreshing and satisfying wraps are a great addition to a gallstone-friendly diet. They are rich in lean protein from tuna, fiber from vegetables, and healthy fats from avocado, all wrapped in a light and nutritious lettuce leaf.

INGREDIENTS:

- 1 can (5 ounces) tuna in water, drained
- 1/4 cup plain Greek yogurt (low-fat or non-fat)
- 1/4 cup chopped celery
- 1/4 cup chopped red onion
- 1/4 cup chopped cucumber
- 1/4 ripe avocado, mashed
- 1 tablespoon lemon juice
- Salt and pepper to taste
- 4 large lettuce leaves (butter lettuce or romaine)

COOKING INSTRUCTIONS:

1. In a bowl, combine tuna, Greek yogurt, celery, red onion, cucumber, mashed avocado, and lemon juice.

2. Season with salt and pepper to taste.

3. Divide the tuna salad evenly among the lettuce leaves.

4. Roll up the lettuce leaves and enjoy!

COOKING TECHNIQUES:

- Vegetables need to be finely chopped for even spread in the salad.
- Ingredients are combined and mixed thoroughly to create a cohesive salad.
- Lettuce leaves are used as a wrap to hold the tuna salad.

NUTRITIONAL VALUES PER SERVING (APPROXIMATE):

- Calories: 200-250 kcal
- Protein: 15-20 g
- Fat: 10-15 g
- Carbohydrates: 5-10 g
- Fiber: 4-6 g

Serving Portion: This recipe makes 2 servings.

Cooking Time: 10 minutes

Prep Time: 10 minutes

This dish is great for the gallstone diet. It is low in fat, high in protein and fiber, and does not include any of the restricted products on the list. Tuna is a lean protein source, while veggies contain vital fiber. Greek yogurt gives richness without the extra fat of mayonnaise, while avocado contains healthful fats.

Additional Tips:

- For extra flavor, add a teaspoon of Dijon mustard or a sprinkle of your favorite herbs and spices to the tuna salad.

- If you like a different type of fish, you can substitute canned salmon or chicken for the tuna.

- You can use any type of lettuce you like, but butter lettuce or romaine work particularly well for wraps.

7. Quinoa and Vegetable Stir-Fry

This delicious and nutritious Quinoa and Vegetable Stir-Fry is a great addition to a gallstone-friendly diet. It's rich in fiber-rich quinoa, colorful vegetables, and lean protein, making it a nutritious and satisfying meal. The meal is low in fat and cholesterol, making it gentle on your gallbladder.

INGREDIENTS:

- 1 cup quinoa
- 2 cups vegetable broth (low-sodium)
- 1 tablespoon olive oil
- 1 onion, chopped
- 2 cloves garlic, minced
- 1 red bell pepper, sliced
- 1 yellow bell pepper, sliced
- 1 zucchini, diced
- 1 cup broccoli florets
- 1/2 cup chopped carrots
- 1/4 cup chopped fresh parsley
- 2 tablespoons soy sauce (low-sodium)
- 1 teaspoon ground ginger
- 1/4 teaspoon black pepper
- Optional: 1/4 cup chopped walnuts or almonds

COOKING INSTRUCTIONS:

1. Rinse quinoa thoroughly and cook according to package instructions using vegetable broth.

2. While quinoa is cooking, heat olive oil in a large pan or wok over medium heat.

3. Add onion and garlic and cook until softened about 3 minutes.

4. Add bell peppers, zucchini, broccoli, and carrots. Stir-fry for 5-7 minutes, or until vegetables are tender-crisp.

5. Stir in cooked quinoa, parsley, soy sauce, ginger, and black pepper.

6. Cook for an additional 2-3 minutes, or until heated through.

7. If desired, sprinkle with chopped walnuts or almonds before serving.

COOKING TECHNIQUES:

- This quick cooking method helps preserve the nutrients and bright colors of the vegetables.

- Rinsing quinoa removes bitterness and cooking it in broth adds flavor.

NUTRITIONAL VALUES PER SERVING (APPROXIMATE):

- Calories: 350-400 kcal

- Protein: 12-15 g

- Fat: 10-15 g

- Carbohydrates: 50-55 g

- Fiber: 10-12 g

Serving Portion: This recipe makes 4 servings.

Cooking Time: 25-30 minutes

Prep Time: 15 minutes

DIET RECIPE NOTE:

This Quinoa and Vegetable Stir-Fry is great for those on a gallstone diet since it avoids fried meals, fatty meats, full-fat dairy, refined grains, and sweetened drinks. It's a healthy and delicious approach to fuel your body while also supporting your gallbladder's health.

_____

_____

_____

_____

_____

8. Chicken and Vegetable Sticks

These chicken and Vegetable Sticks are a delicious and healthy snack or light meal option, perfect for those following a gallstone diet. They are rich in lean protein, fiber, and essential nutrients, making them a satisfying and guilt-free choice.

INGREDIENTS:

- 1 boneless, skinless chicken breast, cut into thin strips

- 1 tablespoon olive oil

- 1/2 teaspoon paprika

- 1/4 teaspoon garlic powder

- 1/4 teaspoon onion powder

- Salt and pepper to taste

- Assorted vegetables (bell peppers, carrots, zucchini, cucumbers), cut into sticks

COOKING INSTRUCTIONS:

1. Heat oven to 400°F (200°C).

2. In a bowl, mix chicken strips with olive oil, paprika, garlic powder, onion powder, salt, and pepper.

3. Spread chicken strips on a baking sheet lined with parchment paper.

4. Bake for 15-20 minutes, or until cooked through.

5. Serve chicken sticks with assorted vegetable sticks for dipping.

COOKING TECHNIQUES:

- Baking the chicken ensures it's cooked through without adding any unhealthy fats.

- Cutting the vegetables into sticks makes them easy to dip and eat.

NUTRITIONAL VALUES PER SERVING (APPROXIMATE):

- Calories: 200 kcal

- Protein: 25 g

- Fat: 8 g

- Carbohydrates: 5 g

- Fiber: 2 g

Serving Portion: This recipe makes 2-3 servings.

Cooking Time: 20 minutes

Prep Time: 10 minutes

These Chicken and Vegetable Sticks are ideal for a gallstone diet. They are low in fat, high in protein, and loaded with fiber from veggies. The dish excludes all of the things you must limit or avoid on a gallstone diet, making it a safe and healthful choice.

Additional Tips:

- You can marinate the chicken in your favorite low-fat marinade for added taste.
- Try with different vegetables like broccoli, cauliflower, or snap peas.
- Serve with a side of hummus or a low-fat yogurt dip for extra taste and protein.
- This recipe can be easily doubled or tripled to make a larger batch for meal prepping.

_____

_____

_____

_____

_____

_____

_____

_____

_____

9. Greek Salad with Grilled Shrimp

This refreshing and pleasant Greek Salad with Grilled Shrimp is a great addition to your gallstone diet. Rich with fresh vegetables, lean protein, and healthy fats, it's a light and satisfying meal that won't burden your gallbladder.

INGREDIENTS:

- 1/2-pound large shrimp, peeled and deveined
- 1 tablespoon olive oil
- 1/2 teaspoon dried oregano
- 1/4 teaspoon salt
- 1/4 teaspoon black pepper
- 4 cups mixed greens (romaine, spinach, or your favorite)
- 1 cucumber, sliced
- 1 red bell pepper, chopped
- 1/2 cup cherry tomatoes, halved
- 1/4 cup Kalamata olives, pitted
- 1/4 cup crumbled feta cheese (low-fat or fat-free options available)

DRESSING:

- 2 tablespoons olive oil
- 2 tablespoons red wine vinegar
- 1 tablespoon lemon juice
- 1/2 teaspoon Dijon mustard
- 1/4 teaspoon dried oregano
- Pinch of salt and pepper

COOKING INSTRUCTIONS:

1. In a bowl, combine shrimp, olive oil, oregano, salt, and pepper. Let marinate for 15 minutes.

2. Heat a grill or grill pan to medium heat. Grill shrimp for 2-3 minutes per side, or until cooked through and pink.

3. In a large bowl, combine mixed greens, cucumber, bell pepper, tomatoes, and olives.

4. In a small bowl, mix olive oil, red wine vinegar, lemon juice, Dijon mustard, oregano, salt, and pepper.

5. Add grilled shrimp to the salad bowl. Sprinkle with dressing and toss to coat. Top with crumbled feta cheese.

COOKING TECHNIQUES:

- Marinating the shrimp helps flavor and tenderness.

- Grilling adds a smoky char and keeps the shrimp lean.

- Mixing the dressing ingredients ensures they are well combined.

NUTRITIONAL VALUES PER SERVING (APPROXIMATE):

- Calories: 350-400 kcal

- Protein: 25-30 g

- Fat: 15-20 g

- Carbohydrates: 10-15 g

- Fiber: 5-7 g

Serving Portion: This recipe makes 2 servings.

Cooking Time: 20 minutes

Prep Time: 15 minutes

DIET RECIPE NOTE:

This Greek Salad with Grilled Shrimp is ideal for a gallstone diet. It's low in saturated fat, high in fiber, and full of lean protein and fresh veggies. It avoids all of the foods that should be limited or avoided on a gallstone diet.

Additional Tips:

- To make this recipe vegetarian, substitute the shrimp with grilled tofu or chickpeas.

- If you don't have a grill, you can bake the shrimp in the oven at 400°F for 8-10 minutes.

- For extra taste, add a sprinkle of fresh herbs like dill or mint to the salad.

10. Vegetable Quinoa Wrap

This Vegetable Quinoa Wrap is a nutritious and satisfying meal option great for those following a gallstone diet. Rich with fiber-rich vegetables, lean protein from quinoa, and healthy fats from avocado, this wrap is not only delicious but also supports gallbladder health.

INGREDIENTS:

- 1 whole-wheat tortilla
- 1/2 cup cooked quinoa
- 1/4 avocado, sliced
- 1/4 cup shredded carrots
- 1/4 cup chopped cucumber
- 1/4 cup chopped bell pepper
- 1/4 cup hummus
- 2-3 leaves of lettuce

COOKING INSTRUCTIONS:

1. Warm the tortilla in a dry pan or microwave.
2. Spread hummus evenly on the tortilla.
3. Layer the cooked quinoa, avocado slices, shredded carrots, chopped cucumber, and bell pepper on top of the hummus.
4. Top with lettuce leaves.
5. Roll the tortilla tightly into a wrap.

COOKING TECHNIQUES:

- Gently warm the tortilla to make it pliable for rolling.
- Create a balanced and tasteful filling by layering the ingredients evenly.
- Roll the tortilla tightly to secure the ingredients and prevent spillage.

NUTRITIONAL VALUES PER SERVING (APPROXIMATE):

- Calories: 350-400 kcal
- Protein: 10-12 g
- Fat: 15-20 g
- Carbohydrates: 40-45 g

- Fiber: 10-12 g

Serving Portion: This recipe makes one serving.

Cooking Time: 5-10 minutes

Prep Time: 10-15 minutes (including cooking quinoa)

DIET RECIPE NOTE:

This Vegetable Quinoa Wrap is ideal for a gallstone diet since it contains fiber-rich veggies, lean protein, and healthy fats. It avoids all of the foods that should be limited or avoided on a gallstone diet. Feel free to add your favorite veggies to the fillings, or sprinkle with low-fat dressing for added taste.

_____

_____

_____

_____

_____

_____

_____

_____

_____

11. Grilled Chicken Salad with Mixed Greens and Balsamic Vinaigrette

This refreshing and tasteful salad is a great addition to a gallstone-friendly diet. It's rich in lean protein from the grilled chicken, fiber from the mixed greens, and healthy fats from the avocado and balsamic vinaigrette. This dish is not only delicious but also supports your gallbladder health.

INGREDIENTS:

- **SALAD:**

  o 4 cups mixed greens (spring mix, spinach, arugula)

  o 1 grilled chicken breast, sliced (seasoned with herbs and spices)

  o 1/2 avocado, diced

  o 1/4 cup cherry tomatoes, halved

  o 1/4 cup cucumber, sliced

BALSAMIC VINAIGRETTE:

  o 2 tablespoons balsamic vinegar

  o 1 tablespoon extra-virgin olive oil

  o 1 teaspoon Dijon mustard

  o 1/2 teaspoon honey or maple syrup (optional)

  o Pinch of salt and pepper

COOKING INSTRUCTIONS:

1. In a small bowl, mix the balsamic vinegar, olive oil, Dijon mustard, honey (if using), salt, and pepper until well combined.

2. In a large bowl, combine the mixed greens, sliced chicken, avocado, cherry tomatoes, and cucumber.

3. Sprinkle the balsamic vinaigrette over the salad and toss gently to coat.

COOKING TECHNIQUES:

- The chicken is grilled for a healthy cooking method that avoids added fats.

- Use a whisk to emulsify the vinaigrette for a smooth and creamy texture.

- Assemble the salad ingredients and toss gently to avoid bruising the greens.

- Calories: 350-400 kcal

- Protein: 25-30 g

- Fat: 15-20 g

- Carbohydrates: 10-15 g

- Fiber: 5-7 g

Serving Portion: This recipe makes one generous serving.

Cooking Time: 15-20 minutes (including grilling time for the chicken)

Prep Time: 10 minutes

DIET RECIPE NOTE:

This Grilled Chicken Salad is a great addition to a gallstone diet. It's low in fat, high in fiber, and steers clear of all the items that should be limited or avoided on a gallstone diet. The grilled chicken provides lean protein, while the mixed greens and avocado include vitamins, minerals, and healthy fats. The balsamic vinaigrette provides a taste without using excessive oil or sugar.

Tips for Newly Diagnosed:

- If you're new to a gallstone diet, this salad is a great starting point. It's easy to digest and can be selected to your liking.

- Be sure to grill or bake the chicken instead of frying it to keep it low in fat.

- Use a light hand with the dressing to avoid adding too much fat to the salad.

- Feel free to add other gallstone-friendly vegetables like bell peppers, carrots, or beets.

12. Quinoa Salad with Cucumber, Tomato, and Lemon Dressing

This refreshing quinoa salad is a great addition to a gallstone-friendly diet. It's rich in fiber from quinoa and vegetables, gives lean protein, and features a light, zesty lemon dressing that avoids the high-fat content often found in creamy dressings.

INGREDIENTS:

- 1 cup quinoa, cooked and cooled
- 1 cucumber, diced
- 1 pint cherry tomatoes, halved
- 1/4 cup chopped fresh parsley
- 1/4 cup chopped fresh mint
- 2 tablespoons extra-virgin olive oil
- 2 tablespoons lemon juice
- 1/2 teaspoon Dijon mustard
- Salt and pepper to taste

COOKING INSTRUCTIONS:

1. In a large bowl, combine the cooked quinoa, diced cucumber, halved cherry tomatoes, parsley, and mint.

2. In a small bowl, mix the olive oil, lemon juice, Dijon mustard, salt, and pepper.

3. Pour the dressing over the salad and toss to combine.

4. Let the salad rest for at least 15 minutes to allow the flavors to meld.

PREP TECHNIQUES:

- Rinse quinoa thoroughly before cooking to remove bitterness. Cook according to package directions.

- Mix the dressing ingredients until emulsified.

NUTRITIONAL VALUES PER SERVING (APPROXIMATE):

- Calories: 250-300 kcal
- Protein: 8-10 g
- Fat: 10-15 g
- Carbohydrates: 30-35 g

- Fiber: 5-7 g

Serving Portion: This recipe makes 4-6 servings.

Cooking Time: 15-20 minutes (mostly for quinoa cooking)

Prep Time: 15 minutes

DIET RECIPE NOTE:

This quinoa salad complements a gallstone-friendly diet. It avoids fried meals, fatty meats, high-fat dairy, refined grains, and sweetened drinks. It is also low in fat, high in fiber, and contains important nutrients. You may increase the nutritional density by using other low-fat, high-fiber veggies such as sliced bell peppers or broccoli.

Tips for Newly Diagnosed:

- If you're new to quinoa, start with a smaller portion to see how your body reacts.

- Feel free to adjust the amount of dressing to your own liking.

- This salad can be made ahead of time and stored in the refrigerator for a convenient meal or snack.

- For added protein, consider topping the salad with grilled chicken or fish (prepared without added fat).

---

13. Veggie Stir-Fry with Brown Rice

This bright Veggie Stir-Fry with Brown Rice is a delicious and nutritious meal that's great for those following a gallstone diet. It's rich in fiber-rich vegetables, lean protein, and complex carbohydrates, making it a satisfying and healthy choice for lunch or dinner.

INGREDIENTS:

- 1 cup brown rice, cooked
- 1 tablespoon olive oil
- 1/2 onion, chopped
- 1 bell pepper (any color), sliced
- 1 cup broccoli florets
- 1/2 cup chopped carrots
- 1/2 cup snap peas or snow peas
- 2 cloves garlic, minced
- 1 tablespoon low-sodium soy sauce or tamari
- 1 teaspoon grated fresh ginger (optional)
- Pinch of red pepper flakes (optional)
- Fresh herbs (cilantro, parsley) for garnish

COOKING INSTRUCTIONS:

1. Heat olive oil in a large pan or wok over medium heat.

2. Add onion and bell pepper and cook until softened about 5 minutes.

3. Add broccoli, carrots, and snap peas and cook until tender-crisp, about 5-7 minutes.

4. Add garlic, soy sauce, ginger (if using), and red pepper flakes (if using) and cook for 1 minute more.

5. Stir in cooked brown rice and heat through.

6. Garnish with fresh herbs and serve hot.

COOKING TECHNIQUES:

- This quick cooking method helps retain the nutrients and bright colors of the vegetables.
- Used to soften the onions and peppers before adding other vegetables.
- Mincing the garlic helps distribute its flavor evenly throughout the dish.

- Calories: 350-400 kcal

- Protein: 10-12 g

- Fat: 5-8 g

- Carbohydrates: 55-60 g

- Fiber: 10-12 g

Serving Portion: This recipe makes 2-3 servings.

Cooking Time: 20-25 minutes

Prep Time: 15 minutes

DIET RECIPE NOTE:

This Veggie Stir-Fry with Brown Rice is a fantastic choice for a gallstone diet since it is low in fat, high in fiber, and does not contain any items that should be limited or avoided. It contains lean protein from veggies and complex carbs from brown rice, which provide steady energy without stressing your gallbladder.

Additional Tips:

- Feel free to use any combination of vegetables you like. Other options include mushrooms, zucchini, asparagus, or Bok choy.

- For added protein, you can stir in some tofu or tempeh during the last few minutes of cooking.

- If you prefer a spicier dish, adjust the amount of red pepper flakes to your taste.

- Serve with a dollop of plain Greek yogurt or a sprinkle of toasted sesame seeds for extra flavor and texture.

14. Pumpkin Soup with Toasted Whole Grain Bread

This creamy and comforting Pumpkin Soup is a great addition to a gallstone-friendly diet. It's rich in fiber, vitamins, and minerals while being low in fat and cholesterol. The addition of toasted whole-grain bread adds a satisfying crunch and extra fiber to help keep your gallbladder healthy.

INGREDIENTS:

- 1 tablespoon olive oil

- 1 onion, chopped

- 2 cloves garlic, minced

- 1 teaspoon grated fresh ginger

- 1/2 teaspoon turmeric powder

- 1/4 teaspoon ground cinnamon

- 1/8 teaspoon ground nutmeg

- Pinch of cayenne pepper (optional)

- 1 small pumpkin or 2 cans (15 ounces each) of pure pumpkin puree

- 4 cups vegetable broth

- Salt and black pepper to taste

- 2 slices whole-grain bread

- Toppings: Pepitas (pumpkin seeds), chopped fresh herbs (parsley, cilantro), a dollop of plain yogurt

COOKING INSTRUCTIONS:

1. Heat olive oil in a large pot over medium heat. Add onion and cook until softened about 5 minutes.

2. Add garlic, ginger, turmeric, cinnamon, nutmeg, and cayenne pepper (if using). Cook for 1 minute more, stirring constantly.

3. Stir in pumpkin puree and vegetable broth. Bring to a boil, then reduce heat and cook for 15 minutes, or until flavors meld.

4. While the soup is cooked, toast whole-grain bread until golden brown.

5. Season soup with salt and pepper to taste.

6. Serve soup hot with toasted bread on the side. Top with pepitas, fresh herbs, and a dollop of yogurt, if desired.

COOKING TECHNIQUES:

- Cooking the onions and spices in olive oil helps their flavor and aroma.

- Gently simmering the soup allows the flavors to meld and develop.

- Toasting the bread adds texture and a nutty flavor.

NUTRITIONAL VALUES PER SERVING (APPROXIMATE):

- Calories: 250-300 kcal

- Protein: 5-7 g

- Fat: 5-8 g

- Carbohydrates: 40-45 g

- Fiber: 10-12 g

Serving Portion: This recipe makes 4 servings.

Cooking Time: 30 minutes

Prep Time: 15 minutes

DIET RECIPE NOTE:

This Pumpkin Soup is great for a gallstone diet since it is low in fat, high in fiber, and does not contain any items that should be limited or avoided. It's also high in vitamins A, C, and potassium. The inclusion of whole-grain bread boosts fiber consumption.

Important Considerations:

- This recipe is naturally low in fat, but avoid adding cream or high-fat toppings to keep it gallstone-friendly.

- For added protein, consider topping the soup with cooked lentils or beans.

- Feel free to adjust the spices to your taste preferences.

15. Italian Sausage and Peppers

This Italian Sausage and Peppers recipe is a tasty and nutritious dish that can be easily adapted to fit a gallstone-friendly diet. By using lean chicken or turkey sausage and focusing on healthy cooking methods, you can enjoy this classic Italian favorite without worrying about triggering gallbladder discomfort.

INGREDIENTS:

- 1-pound lean chicken or turkey sausage (casings removed)
- 2 bell peppers (any color), sliced
- 1 onion, sliced
- 2 cloves garlic, minced
- 1 (14.5-ounce) can of diced tomatoes, undrained
- 1/2 cup low-sodium chicken broth
- 1 teaspoon dried oregano
- 1/2 teaspoon dried basil
- Salt and pepper to taste

COOKING INSTRUCTIONS:

1. Heat a large pan over medium heat. Add the sausage and cook, breaking it up with a spoon, until browned.

2. Add the bell peppers and onion to the pan and cook until softened about 5 minutes.

3. Stir in the garlic, diced tomatoes, chicken broth, oregano, and basil. Season with salt and pepper to taste.

4. Bring the mixture to a simmer and cook for 15-20 minutes, or until the sauce has thickened and the flavors have melded.

5. Serve hot over brown rice or quinoa.

COOKING TECHNIQUES:

- The sausage, peppers, and onions are sautéed in a pan to develop flavor and soften the vegetables.
- The sauce is cooked to thicken and blend the flavors.

NUTRITIONAL VALUES PER SERVING (APPROXIMATE):

- Calories: 300-350 kcal

- Protein: 20-25 g

- Fat: 15-20 g

- Carbohydrates: 10-15 g

- Fiber: 5-7 g

Serving Portion: This recipe makes 4 servings.

Cooking Time: 30-35 minutes

Prep Time: 15 minutes

DIET RECIPE NOTE:

This Italian Sausage and Peppers dish is ideal for a Gallstone diet if made with lean chicken or turkey sausage and a little additional fat. Avoid using fatty pork sausage or cooking with too much oil. Additionally, serving this recipe over brown rice or quinoa provides fiber and complex carbs, which promote gallbladder health.

Tip: For additional flavor, you can add a splash of balsamic vinegar or a pinch of red pepper flakes to the sauce.

Self-Reflection Questions:

1. What are my usual lunch choices, and how well do they align with a gallstone-friendly diet?

_____

_____

_____

_____

2. Am I open to exploring new and healthier lunch options to support my gallbladder health?

_____

_____

3. What are my taste preferences for lunch, and how can I incorporate them into gallstone-friendly meals?

_____

_____

_____

_____

4. How can I plan and prepare nutritious lunches in advance to ensure I make healthy choices even on busy days?

_____

_____

_____

_____

5. What challenges might I face in maintaining a gallstone-friendly diet during lunch, and how can I overcome them?

_____

_____

_____

CHAPTER 5:

GALLSTONE-FRIENDLY DINNER DISHES

1. Baked Salmon with Steamed Broccoli

This Baked Salmon with Steamed Broccoli recipe is a nutritious and flavorful dinner or lunch option that aligns perfectly with a Gallstone-friendly diet. Salmon is a lean protein source rich in omega-3 fatty acids, which can help reduce inflammation and support gallbladder health. Steamed broccoli provides important fiber and vitamins while remaining gentle on the digestive system.

INGREDIENTS:

- 1 (4-6 ounce) salmon fillet, skin-on or skinless
- 1 tablespoon olive oil
- 1/2 lemon, sliced
- Salt and pepper to taste
- 1 cup broccoli florets

COOKING INSTRUCTIONS:

1. Heat oven to 400°F (200°C).
2. Line a baking sheet with parchment paper.
3. Place the salmon fillet on the prepared baking sheet. Sprinkle with olive oil, season with salt and pepper, and top with lemon slices.
4. Bake for 12-15 minutes, or until the salmon is cooked through and flakes easily with a fork.
5. While the salmon is baking, steam the broccoli florets until tender-crisp, about 5-7 minutes.
6. Serve the baked salmon alongside the steamed broccoli.

COOKING TECHNIQUES:

- The salmon is baked in the oven for even cooking and has a tender texture.
- The broccoli is steamed to retain its nutrients and prevent it from becoming greasy or oily.

NUTRITIONAL VALUES PER SERVING (APPROXIMATE):

- Calories: 300-350 kcal
- Protein: 25-30 g

- Fat: 15-20 g (mostly healthy unsaturated fats from the salmon and olive oil)
- Carbohydrates: 5-10 g
- Fiber: 4-6 g

Serving Portion: This recipe makes one serving.

Cooking Time: 15-20 minutes

Prep Time: 5 minutes

DIET RECIPE NOTE:

This dish for Baked Salmon with Steamed Broccoli is ideal for a gallstone diet. It eliminates all things that should be limited or avoided, focusing instead on lean protein, healthy fats, and fiber-rich veggies. The cooking methods are very easy on the digestive tract, lowering the likelihood of gallbladder pain.

Tip: For extra taste, you can sprinkle the salmon with herbs like dill or parsley before baking. You can also add a squeeze of lemon juice to the steamed broccoli for a bright, zesty touch.

_____

_____

_____

_____

_____

2. Grilled Tilapia with Lemon Herb Quinoa

This Grilled Tilapia with Lemon Herb Quinoa recipe is a light, delicious, and nutritious dish great for a gallstone-friendly diet. Tilapia is a lean protein source, and quinoa is a whole grain riches with fiber, both of which are beneficial for gallbladder health. The addition of fresh herbs and lemon juice adds a burst of flavor without relying on unhealthy fats or oils.

INGREDIENTS:

- 4 tilapia fillets
- 1 cup quinoa
- 2 cups low-sodium vegetable broth or water
- 1/4 cup chopped fresh parsley
- 1/4 cup chopped fresh basil
- 1 tablespoon olive oil
- 1 lemon, juiced and zested
- Salt and pepper to taste

COOKING INSTRUCTIONS:

1. Rinse the quinoa thoroughly. Combine it with the vegetable broth (or water) in a saucepan. Bring to a boil, then reduce heat to low, cover, and cook for 15 minutes or until the quinoa is cooked.

2. While the quinoa is cooking, preheat your grill to medium heat.

3. In a small bowl, combine the parsley, basil, olive oil, lemon juice, and lemon zest. Season with salt and pepper to taste.

4. Brush the tilapia fillets with half of the herb mixture.

5. Place the tilapia fillets on the heat grill and cook for 3-4 minutes per side, or until cooked through.

6. Once the quinoa is cooked, fluff it with a fork and stir in the remaining herb mixture.

7. Serve the grilled tilapia with a generous portion of lemon herb quinoa.

COOKING TECHNIQUES:

- Quinoa is simmered in broth or water until cooked.
- Tilapia fillets are grilled for a healthy cooking method.
- Herbs, oil, and lemon are mixed to create a flavorful sauce.

- Calories: 350-400 kcal

- Protein: 30-35 g

- Fat: 10-15 g

- Carbohydrates: 30-35 g

- Fiber: 5-7 g

Serving Portion: This recipe makes 4 servings.

Cooking Time: 20-25 minutes

Prep Time: 10 minutes

DIET RECIPE NOTE:

This Grilled Tilapia with Lemon Herb Quinoa recipe is a great choice for a gallstone diet. It is low in fat, high in protein and fiber, and avoids all the foods to limit or avoid on a gallstone diet. The grilling method helps keep the fat level low, and the quinoa provides a good source of complex carbohydrates. The fresh herbs and lemon juice provide flavor without adding extra fat or calories.

Tip: To add more vegetables to this meal, consider grilling or roasting some asparagus, zucchini, or bell peppers alongside the tilapia.

_____

_____

_____

_____

_____

3. Vegetable Curry with Basmati Rice

This Vegetable Curry with Basmati Rice recipe is a delicious and nourishing option for those following a gallstone diet. Rich in vegetables and aromatic spices, it is a low-fat, high-fiber dish that supports gallbladder health. The use of coconut milk adds richness and creaminess without being overly heavy.

INGREDIENTS:

- 1 tablespoon olive oil
- 1 onion, chopped
- 2 cloves garlic, minced
- 1 tablespoon curry powder
- 1 teaspoon turmeric
- 1/2 teaspoon cumin
- 1/4 teaspoon cayenne pepper (optional)
- 1 cup chopped vegetables (broccoli, cauliflower, carrots, potatoes, peas)
- 1 (14-ounce) can of diced tomatoes, undrained
- 1 (13.5-ounce) can lite coconut milk
- 1/2 cup chopped cilantro
- Salt and pepper to taste
- 1 cup basmati rice, cooked according to package directions

COOKING INSTRUCTIONS:

1. Heat the olive oil in a large pot or Dutch oven over medium heat. Add the onion and cook until softened about 5 minutes.

2. Add the garlic, curry powder, turmeric, cumin, and cayenne pepper (if using). Cook for 1 minute more, stirring constantly.

3. Add the chopped vegetables, diced tomatoes, and coconut milk to the pot. Stir to combine.

4. Bring the mixture to a boil, then reduce heat to low, cover, and simmer for 20-25 minutes, or until the vegetables are tender.

5. Stir in the chopped cilantro, salt, and pepper to taste.

6. Serve the vegetable curry hot over the cooked basmati rice.

COOKING TECHNIQUES:

- Onions and spices are sautéed in olive oil to help their flavor.

- The curry is simmered to meld the flavors and cook the vegetables.

NUTRITIONAL VALUES PER SERVING (APPROXIMATE):

- Calories: 400-450 kcal

- Protein: 10-12 g

- Fat: 15-20 g

- Carbohydrates: 50-55 g

- Fiber: 10-12 g

Serving Portion: This recipe makes 4 servings.

Cooking Time: 30-35 minutes

Prep Time: 15 minutes

DIET RECIPE NOTE:

This Vegetable Curry with Basmati Rice dish is ideal for a gallstone diet since it is low in fat and high in fiber. It avoids all of the foods that are restricted or avoided on a gallstone diet. Use mild coconut milk to keep the fat content low. This dish is also quite adaptable, so feel free to substitute any mix of your favorite vegetables.

Tip: If you want to make this recipe vegan, you can substitute the lite coconut milk with a plant-based alternative, such as soy milk or almond milk.

4. Baked Chicken Breast with Roasted Sweet Potatoes and Green Beans

This Baked Chicken Breast with Roasted Sweet Potatoes and Green Beans recipe is a complete, balanced, and delicious meal that aligns greatly with a Gallstone-friendly diet. It has lean protein from the chicken breast, fiber-rich sweet potatoes, and antioxidant-rich green beans. The baking method ensures a low-fat preparation, making it gentle on your gallbladder.

INGREDIENTS:

- 2 boneless, skinless chicken breasts
- 2 medium sweet potatoes, peeled and diced
- 1-pound green beans, trimmed
- 2 tablespoons olive oil
- 1 teaspoon paprika
- 1/2 teaspoon garlic powder
- 1/4 teaspoon dried thyme
- Salt and pepper to taste

COOKING INSTRUCTIONS:

1. Heat oven to 400°F (200°C).
2. In a bowl, toss the sweet potatoes with 1 tablespoon of olive oil, paprika, garlic powder, thyme, salt, and pepper. Spread them out on a baking sheet.
3. In another bowl, toss the green beans with the remaining olive oil and season with salt and pepper.
4. Place the chicken breasts on the baking sheet with the sweet potatoes.
5. Bake for 20-25 minutes, or until the chicken is cooked through and the sweet potatoes are soft.
6. Add the green beans to the baking sheet during the last 10 minutes of cooking.
7. Serve hot.

COOKING TECHNIQUES:

- The chicken, sweet potatoes, and green beans are roasted in the oven for a healthy and spicy cooking method.
- Vegetables are tossed with olive oil and seasonings for even distribution.

NUTRITIONAL VALUES PER SERVING (APPROXIMATE):

- Calories: 400-450 kcal

- Protein: 30-35 g

- Fat: 15-20 g

- Carbohydrates: 35-40 g

- Fiber: 10-12 g

Serving Portion: This recipe makes 2 servings.

Cooking Time: 30-35 minutes

Prep Time: 15 minutes

DIET RECIPE NOTE:

This dish for Baked Chicken Breast with Roasted Sweet Potatoes and Green Beans is great for those following a gallstone diet. It is low in fat and high in fiber, with no fried meals, fatty meats, full-fat dairy, refined cereals, or sweetened drinks. The lean protein from the chicken, along with the abundance of veggies, makes for a healthy and fulfilling dinner that promotes gallbladder health.

Tip: To add more flavor, you can marinate the chicken breasts in a mixture of lemon juice, herbs, and spices before baking.

_____

_____

_____

_____

_____

5. Zucchini Noodles with Tomato Basil Sauce

This Zucchini Noodles with Tomato Basil Sauce recipe is a light, refreshing, and spicy meal perfect for a gallstone-friendly diet. Zucchini noodles, also known as *"zoodles,"* *are a low-calorie*, low-carb option to traditional pasta, making them a great choice for individuals managing gallbladder health. The tomato basil sauce is made with fresh ingredients and avoids heavy creams or cheeses, which can trigger gallbladder discomfort.

INGREDIENTS:

- 2-3 medium zucchinis
- 1 tablespoon olive oil
- 3 cloves garlic, minced
- 1 (28-ounce) can crushed tomatoes
- 1/2 cup chopped fresh basil
- Salt and pepper to taste

COOKING INSTRUCTIONS:

1. Use a spiralizer or vegetable peeler to create zucchini noodles.

2. Heat the olive oil in a large pan over medium heat. Add the garlic and cook until aroma, about 30 seconds.

3. Add the crushed tomatoes and basil to the pan. Season with salt and pepper to taste. Bring to a simmer and cook for 10-15 minutes, or until the sauce has thickened.

4. Add the zucchini noodles to the sauce and toss to coat. Cook for 2-3 minutes, or until the noodles are tender-crisp.

5. Serve immediately.

COOKING TECHNIQUES:

- Zucchinis are spiralized to create noodle-like strands.
- Garlic is sautéed in olive oil to help flavor.
- Tomato sauce is simmered to thicken and develop taste.
- Zucchini noodles are tossed with the sauce to coat evenly.

NUTRITIONAL VALUES PER SERVING (APPROXIMATE):

- Calories: 150-200 kcal
- Protein: 5-7 g
- Fat: 5-8 g

- Carbohydrates: 20-25 g

- Fiber: 4-6 g

Serving Portion: This recipe makes 2-3 servings.

Cooking Time: 20 minutes

Prep Time: 10 minutes

DIET RECIPE NOTE:

This Zucchini Noodles with Tomato Basil Sauce dish is suitable for a gallstone diet. It is low in fat, high in fiber, and does not contain any of the foods that should be limited or avoided on a gallstone diet. Zucchini noodles are a healthier alternative to classic pasta, and the fresh tomato basil sauce adds taste without any extra fat or dairy.

Tips:

- For added protein, you can top the meal with grilled chicken or shrimp.

- If you don't have a spiralizer, you can use a vegetable peeler to create wide zucchini ribbons.

- Is good to add other vegetables to the sauce, such as chopped bell peppers or mushrooms.

- For a spicier dish, add a pinch of red pepper flakes to the sauce.

_____

_____

_____

_____

_____

6. Cod with a Citrus and Herb Crust

This Cod with a Citrus and Herb Crust recipe is a tasteful and healthy option for those following a gallstone diet. It has lean, flaky cod fish baked with a good aromatic crust made from herbs, citrus zest, and whole-wheat breadcrumbs. This meal is not only delicious but also rich in nutrients and low in fat, making it ideal for supporting gallbladder health.

INGREDIENTS:

- 4 cod fillets (about 6 ounces each)
- 1/4 cup whole-wheat breadcrumbs
- 1/4 cup chopped fresh parsley
- 1/4 cup chopped fresh dill
- 1 tablespoon lemon zest
- 1 tablespoon orange zest
- 2 cloves garlic, minced
- 2 tablespoons olive oil
- Salt and pepper to taste

COOKING INSTRUCTIONS:

1. Heat oven to 400°F (200°C).

2. In a small bowl, combine breadcrumbs, parsley, dill, lemon zest, orange zest, garlic, olive oil, salt, and pepper. Mix well.

3. Place the cod fillets on a baking sheet lined with parchment paper.

4. Press the herb mixture onto the top of each fillet, ensuring an even coating.

5. Bake for 12-15 minutes, or until the fish is cooked through and the crust is golden brown.

COOKING TECHNIQUES:

- The cod is baked in the oven for a healthy cooking method that doesn't require added fats.
- Herbs and garlic are chopped for flavor and aroma.
- The crust ingredients are mixed to create a flavorful coating.

NUTRITIONAL VALUES PER SERVING (APPROXIMATE):

- Calories: 250-300 kcal

- Protein: 30-35 g

- Fat: 5-8 g

- Carbohydrates: 10-15 g

- Fiber: 2-3 g

Serving Portion: This recipe makes 4 servings.

Cooking Time: 12-15 minutes

Prep Time: 10 minutes

DIET RECIPE NOTE:

This Cod with Citrus and Herb Crust is ideal for a gallstone diet. It includes lean protein (cod), whole grains (whole-wheat breadcrumbs), and healthy fats (olive oil), but avoids fried dishes, fatty meats, and full-fat dairy. The fresh herbs and citrus zest add flavor without using high-fat components.

Tips:

- Is good to substitute other fresh herbs like thyme or rosemary based on your preference.

- For more flavor, sprinkle a bit of lemon juice over the fish before serving.

- Serve this meal with a side of steamed vegetables or a mixed green salad for a complete and balanced meal.

7. Veggie Lasagna with Eggplant and Zucchini

This Veggie Lasagna with Eggplant and Zucchini is a delicious and healthy option to traditional lasagna, making it a great addition to a gallstone-friendly diet. It's rich in fiber-rich vegetables, lean protein from ricotta cheese, and a spicy tomato sauce, all while avoiding high-fat ingredients like meat and full-fat cheese.

INGREDIENTS:

- 1 large eggplant, sliced thinly
- 2-3 zucchinis, sliced thinly
- 1 tablespoon olive oil
- 1 onion, chopped
- 3 cloves garlic, minced
- 1 (28-ounce) can crushed tomatoes
- 1/2 cup chopped fresh basil
- 1 cup part-skim ricotta cheese
- 1/2 cup grated Parmesan cheese
- 9 lasagna noodles (no-boil or regular)
- Salt and pepper to taste

COOKING INSTRUCTIONS:

1. Heat oven to 375°F (190°C).

2. Brush eggplant and zucchini slices with olive oil and season with salt and pepper. Grill or roast until softened and slightly browned.

3. While the vegetables are cooking, heat olive oil in a large pan over medium heat. Add onion and cook until softened, then add garlic and cook for another minute.

4. Stir in the crushed tomatoes and basil. Season with salt and pepper and cook for 15 minutes.

5. In a bowl, combine ricotta and Parmesan cheese.

6. In a 9x13-inch baking bowl, spread a thin layer of tomato sauce. Top with a layer of lasagna noodles, followed by a layer of eggplant and zucchini, a layer of ricotta mixture, and a layer of tomato sauce.

Repeat layers until all ingredients are used, ending with a layer of tomato sauce.

7. Cover the bowl with foil and bake for 30 minutes. Uncover and bake for an additional 15 minutes, or until the cheese is melted and bubbly.

8. Let stand for 10 minutes before serving.

COOKING TECHNIQUES:

- Eggplant and zucchini are grilled or roasted for a healthier cooking method.

- Onion and garlic are sautéed to help flavor.

- Tomato sauce is simmered to thicken and develop taste.

- Ingredients are layered in a baking bowl to create the lasagna.

- Lasagna is baked until the cheese is melted and bubbly.

NUTRITIONAL VALUES PER SERVING (APPROXIMATE):

- Calories: 300-350 kcal

- Protein: 15-20 g

- Fat: 10-15 g

- Carbohydrates: 30-35 g

- Fiber: 8-10 g

Serving Portion: This recipe makes 8-10 servings.

Cooking Time: 45 minutes

Prep Time: 30 minutes

DIET RECIPE NOTE:

This Veggie Lasagna with Eggplant and Zucchini is appropriate for the gallstone diet. It's full of veggies, made with part-skim ricotta and parmesan cheese to lower fat, and free of fried meals, fatty meats, full-fat dairy, and processed carbohydrates. The lasagna noodles used are either no-boil or regular, which are both diet-friendly.

Tip: To make this recipe even healthier, you can use whole-wheat lasagna noodles for added fiber.

8. Moroccan Chicken with Couscous

This Moroccan Chicken with Couscous recipe is a tasteful and healthy meal that is well-suited for a gallstone-friendly diet. It has lean chicken breast, a variety of vegetables, and whole-grain couscous, all of which are recommended for those with gallbladder concerns. The warm spices and aromatic taste of Morocco add depth to this meal without relying on unhealthy fats or ingredients.

INGREDIENTS:

- 1-pound boneless, skinless chicken breasts, cut into 1-inch pieces
- 1 tablespoon olive oil
- 1 onion, chopped
- 2 cloves garlic, minced
- 1 teaspoon ground cumin
- 1 teaspoon ground coriander
- 1/2 teaspoon ground turmeric
- 1/4 teaspoon cayenne pepper (optional)
- 1 (14.5-ounce) can of diced tomatoes, undrained
- 1 cup low-sodium chicken broth
- 1 cup couscous
- 1/2 cup chopped dried apricots
- 1/4 cup chopped fresh cilantro
- Salt and pepper to taste

COOKING INSTRUCTIONS:

1. Heat the olive oil in a large pan over medium heat. Add the chicken and cook until browned on all sides.

2. Add the onion and cook until softened, about 5 minutes. Stir in the garlic, cumin, coriander, turmeric, and cayenne pepper (if using). Cook for 1 minute more.

3. Add the diced tomatoes, chicken broth, and dried apricots to the pan. Bring to a simmer and cook for 15 minutes, or until

the chicken is cooked through and the sauce has thickened.

4. While the chicken is cooking, prepare the couscous according to package instructions.

5. Fluff the couscous with a fork and stir in the chopped cilantro.

6. Serve the Moroccan chicken over the couscous.

COOKING TECHNIQUES:

- Chicken and vegetables are sautéed in olive oil to develop taste.
- The sauce is simmered to thicken and blend the flavors.

NUTRITIONAL VALUES PER SERVING (APPROXIMATE):

- Calories: 400-450 kcal
- Protein: 30-35 g
- Fat: 10-15 g
- Carbohydrates: 40-45 g
- Fiber: 5-7 g

Serving Portion: This recipe makes 4 servings.

Cooking Time: 30 minutes

Prep Time: 15 minutes

DIET RECIPE NOTE:

This Moroccan Chicken with Couscous dish is ideal for those on a gallstone diet. It contains lean protein, balanced carbs, and various veggies. The dish is low in fat and does not include fried dishes, fatty meats, full-fat dairy, or processed cereals. The dried apricots give both sweetness and fiber.

Tip: For a spicier bowl, you can increase the amount of cayenne pepper or add chopped chili pepper to the sauce. To add more vegetables, consider adding diced carrots or zucchini to the pan along with the onions.

9. Vegan Chili with Sweet Potato and Black Beans

This delicious and nutritious Vegan Chili with Sweet Potato and Black Beans is a great addition to a gallstone-friendly diet. It's rich in fiber-rich vegetables, lean plant-based protein, and warming spices, all of which support gallbladder health. This chili is also naturally low in fat and cholesterol, making it a delicious and nutritious option for those managing gallstones.

INGREDIENTS:

- 1 tablespoon olive oil
- 1 onion, chopped
- 2 cloves garlic, minced
- 1 large sweet potato, peeled and diced
- 1 red bell pepper, chopped
- 1 jalapeno pepper, seeded and minced (optional)
- 1 tablespoon chili powder
- 1 teaspoon ground cumin
- 1/2 teaspoon smoked paprika
- 1/4 teaspoon cayenne pepper (optional)
- 1 (28-ounce) can have diced tomatoes, undrained
- 1 (15-ounce) can black beans, rinsed and drained
- 1 cup vegetable broth
- Salt and pepper to taste
- Optional toppings: chopped cilantro, avocado slices, lime wedges

COOKING INSTRUCTIONS:

1. Heat the olive oil in a large pot or Dutch oven over medium heat. Add the onion and cook until softened about 5 minutes.

2. Add the garlic, sweet potato, bell pepper, and jalapeno (if using) to the pot. Cook, stirring mostly, for 5-7 minutes, or until the vegetables start to soften.

3. Stir in the chili powder, cumin, smoked paprika, and cayenne pepper (if using).

Cook for 1 minute more to toast the spices.

4. Add the diced tomatoes, black beans, and vegetable broth to the pot. Bring to a boil, then reduce heat and cook for 20-25 minutes, or until the sweet potato is tender and the chili has thickened.

5. Season with salt and pepper to taste.

6. Serve hot, topped with your desired toppings.

COOKING TECHNIQUES:

- Onions, garlic, and vegetables are sautéed in olive oil to help flavor.
- Chili is cooked to thicken and blend the flavors.

NUTRITIONAL VALUES PER SERVING (APPROXIMATE):

- Calories: 350-400 kcal
- Protein: 15-20 g | Fat: 5-8 g
- Carbohydrates: 50-60 g
- Fiber: 15-20 g

Serving Portion: This recipe makes 6-8 servings.

Cooking Time: 30-35 minutes

Prep Time: 15 minutes

DIET RECIPE NOTE:

This Vegan Chili with Sweet Potato and Black Beans is ideal for a gallstone diet. It contains fiber from sweet potatoes, black beans, and vegetables, which can help manage cholesterol and improve good digestion. It is also low in fat and entirely plant-based, making it a heart-healthy and gallbladder-friendly choice.

Tips:

- For a spicier chili, increase the amount of jalapeno or cayenne pepper.
- To make this recipe in a slow cooker, combine all ingredients in the slow cooker and cook on low for 6-8 hours or on high for 3-4 hours.
- Is good to add other vegetables like corn, carrots, or zucchini to the chili.
- This chili freezes well, so you can make a big batch and enjoy it for multiple meals.

10. Turkey Meatballs with Spaghetti Squash

This Turkey Meatballs with Spaghetti Squash recipe is a delicious and nutritious option for local spaghetti and meatballs. It's great for those following a gallstone diet as it's low in fat, high in fiber, and rich in protein. Spaghetti squash, a low-calorie, and low-carb veggie, replaces regular pasta, while lean ground turkey provides a healthy protein source.

INGREDIENTS:

- 1 medium spaghetti squash

- 1 pound ground turkey

- 1/2 cup breadcrumbs (whole wheat or gluten-free)

- 1/4 cup grated Parmesan cheese

- 1 egg

- 1/4 cup chopped fresh parsley

- 1/4 cup chopped fresh basil

- 2 cloves garlic, minced

- 1/2 teaspoon dried oregano

- Salt and pepper to taste

- 1 jar (24 ounces) marinara sauce (low-sodium, no added sugar)

- 1 tablespoon olive oil

COOKING INSTRUCTIONS:

1. Heat oven to 400°F (200°C). Cut the spaghetti squash in half lengthwise and scoop out the seeds. Place the squash halves cut-side down on a baking sheet and bake for 30-40 minutes, or until tender.

2. While the squash is baking, combine the ground turkey, breadcrumbs, Parmesan cheese, egg, parsley, basil, garlic, oregano, salt, and pepper in a large bowl. Mix well with your hands.

3. Form the mixture into small meatballs.

4. Heat the olive oil in a large pan over medium heat. Add the meatballs and cook until browned on all sides.

5. Pour the marinara sauce over the meatballs and bring to a cook. Cook for

10-15 minutes, or until the meatballs are cooked through.

6. Once the spaghetti squash is cooked, use a fork to scrape the flesh into strands.

7. Divide the spaghetti squash among plates and top with meatballs and sauce.

COOKING TECHNIQUES:

- Spaghetti squash is roasted in the oven until tender.

- Meatball ingredients are mixed by hand.

- Meatballs are browned in olive oil.

- Meatballs are cooked in marinara sauce until cooked through.

NUTRITIONAL VALUES PER SERVING (APPROXIMATE):

- Calories: 400-450 kcal

- Protein: 30-35 g

- Fat: 15-20 g

- Carbohydrates: 30-35 g

- Fiber: 5-7 g

Serving Portion: This recipe makes 4 servings.

Cooking Time: 45-50 minutes

Prep Time: 20 minutes

DIET RECIPE NOTE:

This Turkey Meatballs with Spaghetti Squash dish is appropriate for a gallstone diet. It eliminates all of the things that should be limited or avoided on a gallstone diet, including fried meals, fatty meats, full-fat dairy, refined cereals, and sugary beverages. The spaghetti squash contains fiber, and the lean ground turkey is a healthy protein alternative. Using a low-sodium marinara sauce with no additional sugar helps make the dish healthful and tasty.

11. Stuffed Bell Peppers with Ground Turkey and Quinoa

This Stuffed Bell Peppers with Ground Turkey and Quinoa recipe is a nutritious and delicious meal that aligns greatly with a gallstone-friendly diet. Bell peppers are rich in vitamins and fiber, while ground turkey gives a lean protein source. Quinoa, a whole grain, provides additional fiber and essential nutrients, promoting healthy digestion and gallbladder function.

INGREDIENTS:

- 4 bell peppers (any color)
- 1 pound ground turkey (93% lean or leaner)
- 1/2 cup quinoa, cooked
- 1/2 cup chopped onion
- 1/2 cup chopped mushrooms
- 2 cloves garlic, minced
- 1 (14.5-ounce) can of diced tomatoes, undrained
- 1/4 cup chopped fresh parsley
- 1 teaspoon dried oregano
- 1/2 teaspoon salt
- 1/4 teaspoon black pepper

COOKING INSTRUCTIONS:

1. Heat oven to 375°F (190°C).

2. Cut the tops off the bell peppers and remove the seeds and membranes.

3. In a large pan over medium heat, brown the ground turkey.

4. Add the onion, mushrooms, and garlic to the pan and cook until softened.

5. Stir in the cooked quinoa, diced tomatoes, parsley, oregano, salt, and pepper.

6. Fill each bell pepper with the turkey and quinoa mixture.

7. Place the stuffed peppers in a baking bowl and add 1/4 inch of water to the bottom of the bowl.

8. Bake for 30-35 minutes, or until the peppers are tender and the filling is heated through.

COOKING TECHNIQUES:

- Ground turkey, onions, mushrooms, and garlic are sautéed for taste.
- Stuffed peppers are baked in the oven until tender.

NUTRITIONAL VALUES PER SERVING (APPROXIMATE):

- Calories: 350-400 kcal
- Protein: 25-30 g
- Fat: 15-20 g
- Carbohydrates: 25-30 g
- Fiber: 5-7 g

Serving Portion: This recipe makes 4 servings.

Cooking Time: 30-35 minutes

Prep Time: 20 minutes

DIET RECIPE NOTE:

This dish for Stuffed Bell Peppers is great for those on a gallstone diet. It contains lean ground turkey, fiber-rich quinoa, and veggies while avoiding any foods that should be limited or avoided on a gallstone diet. This dish is baked rather than fried, which further reduces fat content.

Tips:

- To reduce sodium, use low-sodium or no-salt-added diced tomatoes.
- You can substitute ground chicken or lean ground beef for ground turkey.
- For more taste, top the peppers with a sprinkle of grated parmesan cheese (optional, as dairy should be limited).
- Serve with a side salad for a complete and balanced meal.

12. Butternut Squash Risotto

This Butternut Squash Risotto recipe is a creamy, comforting, and delicious meal that can be adapted to be gallstone-friendly. By using low-sodium vegetable broth, a minimal quantity of olive oil, and omitting cheese, you can enjoy this classic Italian meal without triggering gallbladder discomfort. The natural sweetness of the butternut squash adds depth of taste, while the Arborio rice creates a creamy texture.

INGREDIENTS:

- 1 medium butternut squash, peeled, seeded, and diced

- 1 tablespoon olive oil

- 1 small onion, finely chopped

- 2 cloves garlic, minced

- 1 cup Arborio rice

- 4 cups low-sodium vegetable broth, warmed

- 1/4 cup dry white wine (optional)

- 1/4 cup grated Parmesan cheese (optional, omit for strict gallstone diet)

- Salt and pepper to taste

- Fresh herbs for garnish (optional)

COOKING INSTRUCTIONS:

1. Heat oven to 400°F (200°C). Toss the diced butternut squash with a sprinkle of olive oil, salt, and pepper. Roast for 20-25 minutes, or until tender.

2. While the squash is roasting, heat the olive oil in a large pan or pot over medium heat. Add the onion and cook until softened about 5 minutes. Add the garlic and cook for another minute.

3. Stir in the Arborio rice and cook for 1-2 minutes, until toasted.

4. Add the white wine (if using) and cook until evaporated.

5. Begin adding the warm vegetable broth, one cup at a time, stirring constantly and allowing each cup to absorb before adding the next. Continue until the rice is creamy and al dente, about 20-25 minutes.

6. Stir in the roasted butternut squash. If you want, stir in the Parmesan cheese. Season with salt and pepper to taste.

7. Garnish with fresh herbs, if desired, and serve immediately.

- Butternut squash is roasted to help its sweetness and tastiness.
- Onion and garlic are sautéed to develop taste.
- Arborio rice is cooked in broth to create a creamy texture.

- Calories: 350-400 kcal
- Protein: 10-12 g
- Fat: 10-15 g
- Carbohydrates: 50-60 g
- Fiber: 5-7 g

Serving Portion: This recipe makes 4 servings.

Cooking Time: 45-50 minutes

Prep Time: 20 minutes

This Butternut Squash Risotto dish is readily modified to be gallstone-friendly. To reduce the fat level, omit the Parmesan cheese and use low-sodium vegetable broth instead. The butternut squash adds natural sweetness and vitamins, while the Arborio rice provides complex carbs and fiber, making this a nutritious and fulfilling food for those with problems with the gallbladder.

Tip: For more taste, you can add a pinch of nutmeg or sage to the risotto while it's cooking.

13. Lentil Stew with Kale and Potatoes

This delicious and nutritious Lentil Stew with Kale and Potatoes is a great addition to a gallstone-friendly diet. Lentils are a great source of protein and fiber, while kale is rich in vitamins and minerals. Potatoes add substance and make this a satisfying meal. The stew is cooked with simple ingredients and avoids fatty meats, full-fat dairy, and refined grains, making it a healthy and delicious option for managing gallbladder health.

INGREDIENTS:

- 1 tablespoon olive oil
- 1 medium onion, chopped
- 2 cloves garlic, minced
- 1 teaspoon salt, divided
- 1/2 teaspoon black pepper, divided
- 3 cups low-sodium vegetable broth
- 1 (14.5-ounce) can have diced tomatoes, undrained
- 1 cup red lentils, rinsed
- 4 cups chopped kale
- 2 medium potatoes, peeled and cubed
- Optional: 1/4 cup chopped fresh parsley for garnish

COOKING INSTRUCTIONS:

1. Heat the olive oil in a large pot over medium heat. Add the onion and cook until softened about 5 minutes.

2. Add garlic, 1/2 teaspoon salt, and 1/4 teaspoon pepper. Cook for 30 seconds more.

3. Stir in the broth, tomatoes, lentils, potatoes, and the remaining salt and pepper. Bring to a boil, then reduce heat to low, cover, and cook for 20-25 minutes, or until lentils and potatoes are soft.

4. Stir in the kale and cook until wilted, about 5 minutes more.

5. Ladle into bowls and garnish with parsley, as you want.

COOKING TECHNIQUES:

- Onions and garlic are sautéed in olive oil to help flavor.

- Lentils, potatoes, and kale are cooked in broth until soft.

- Calories: 350-400 kcal

- Protein: 15-20 g

- Fat: 5-8 g

- Carbohydrates: 50-55 g

- Fiber: 15-20 g

Serving Portion: This recipe makes 4-6 servings.

Cooking Time: 40-45 minutes

Prep Time: 15 minutes

DIET RECIPE NOTE:

This lentil stew with kale and potatoes is ideal for a gallstone diet. It has fiber from lentils, kale, and potatoes and is low in fat. It avoids all of the items that should be limited or avoided on a gallstone diet. This hearty stew is a nutritious and filling meal that might aid with gallbladder health.

Tip: For a creamier texture, you can blend a portion of the stew before adding the kale.

_____

_____

_____

_____

_____

14. Eggplant Parmesan with Low-Fat Mozzarella

Eggplant Parmesan is a sweet Italian meal, but it can often be heavy and high in fat. This modified recipe transforms it into a lighter, healthier option that is suitable for a gallstone-friendly diet. By using baked eggplant instead of fried, and opting for low-fat mozzarella, you can enjoy the taste of this classic meal without compromising your gallbladder health.

INGREDIENTS:

- 2 medium eggplants, sliced into 1/2-inch rounds
- 1/2 cup grated Parmesan cheese
- 1 cup low-fat mozzarella cheese, shredded
- 1 (28-ounce) can crushed tomatoes
- 1/2 cup chopped fresh basil
- 2 cloves garlic, minced
- 1 tablespoon olive oil
- Salt and pepper to taste

COOKING INSTRUCTIONS:

1. Heat oven to 400°F (200°C).

2. Brush eggplant slices with olive oil and season with salt and pepper. Arrange on the baking sheet and bake for 20 minutes, flipping halfway through.

3. While the eggplant is baking, prepare the sauce. In a saucepan, heat the olive oil over medium heat. Add the garlic and cook until aroma, about 30 seconds.

4. Add the crushed tomatoes and basil to the saucepan. Season with salt and pepper to taste. Bring to a simmer and cook for 10-15 minutes, or until the sauce has thickened.

5. In a baking bowl, layer the eggplant slices, tomato sauce, and mozzarella cheese. Repeat layers, ending with mozzarella.

6. Sprinkle the top with Parmesan cheese.

7. Bake for 20-25 minutes, or until the cheese is melted and bubbly.

8. Let cool slightly before serving.

COOKING TECHNIQUES:

- Eggplant is baked instead of fried to reduce fat content.

- Garlic is sautéed in olive oil to help flavor.

- Tomato sauce is cooked to thicken and develop taste.

- Ingredients are layered in a baking dish for even cooking.

NUTRITIONAL VALUES PER SERVING (APPROXIMATE):

- Calories: 250-300 kcal

- Protein: 15-20 g

- Fat: 10-15 g

- Carbohydrates: 20-25 g

- Fiber: 5-7 g

Serving Portion: This recipe makes 4-6 servings.

Cooking Time: 45-50 minutes

Prep Time: 20 minutes

DIET RECIPE NOTE:

This Eggplant Parmesan with Low-Fat Mozzarella is acceptable for a gallstone diet since it is baked, not fried, and contains low-fat cheese. It eliminates all of the foods that should be limited or avoided on a gallstone diet, making it a tasty and healthful solution for those maintaining gallbladder health.

Tip: For more boost of taste and fiber, consider adding chopped vegetables like zucchini, spinach, or mushrooms to the tomato sauce.

15. Sautéed Shrimp with Garlic and Herbs over Zoodles

This Sautéed Shrimp with Garlic and Herbs over Zoodles recipe is a light, delicious, and nutritious meal perfect for a gallstone-friendly diet. Shrimp is a low-fat, high-protein seafood option, while zucchini noodles (zoodles) are a low-calorie, low-carb option to traditional pasta. The garlic and herbs add taste without the need for heavy sauces or unhealthy fats.

INGREDIENTS:

- 1-pound large shrimp, peeled and deveined
- 2-3 medium zucchinis
- 2 tablespoons olive oil
- 4 cloves garlic, minced
- 1/4 cup chopped fresh parsley
- 1/4 cup chopped fresh dill
- 1 tablespoon lemon juice
- Salt and pepper to taste

COOKING INSTRUCTIONS:

1. Use a spiralizer or vegetable peeler to create zucchini noodles (zoodles). Put them aside.

2. Heat the olive oil in a large pan over medium heat. Add the shrimp and cook for 2-3 minutes per side or until pink and opaque. Remove the shrimp from the pan and put them aside.

3. Add the garlic to the pan and cook until aromatic, about 30 seconds.

4. Add the zoodles to the pan and cook for 2-3 minutes, or until tender-crisp.

5. Return the shrimp to the pan and stir in the parsley, dill, and lemon juice. Season with salt and pepper to taste.

6. Serve immediately.

COOKING TECHNIQUES:

- Zucchinis are spiralized to create noodle-like strands.
- Shrimp and garlic are sautéed in olive oil to help taste.

- Zoodles, shrimp, and herbs are tossed together to combine taste.

NUTRITIONAL VALUES PER SERVING (APPROXIMATE):

- Calories: 250-300 kcal | Protein: 25-30 g

- Fat: 10-15 g

- Carbohydrates: 10-15 g | Fiber: 3-5 g

Serving Portion: This recipe makes 2-3 servings.

Cooking Time: 15-20 minutes

Prep Time: 10 minutes

DIET RECIPE NOTE:

This Sautéed Shrimp with Garlic and Herbs over Zoodles dish is suitable for a gallstone diet. It is low in fat, rich in protein, and contains none of the items that should be limited or avoided on a gallstone diet. The shrimp provides a lean protein source, and the zoodles provide a low-calorie, low-carb alternative to regular pasta. Garlic, herbs, and lemon juice add taste without the need for heavy sauces or unhealthy fats.

Tip: For a more taste boost, you can add a pinch of red pepper flakes or a sprinkle of balsamic vinegar to the dish.

Self-Reflection Questions:

1. What are my typical dinner choices, and how well do they align with a gallstone-friendly diet?

_____

_____

_____

_____

_____

2. Am I willing to explore new and healthier dinner options to support my gallbladder health?

_____

_____

3. What are my personal preferences for dinner taste and cuisines, and how can I incorporate them into gallstone-friendly meals?

_____

_____

_____

_____

4. How can I plan and prepare nutritious dinners in advance to ensure I make healthy choices even on busy evenings?

_____

_____

_____

_____

5. What challenges might I face in maintaining a gallstone-friendly diet during dinner, and how can I overcome them (e.g., eating out, social gatherings)

_____

_____

CHAPTER 6:

GALLSTONE-FRIENDLY SNACKS & DESSERTS

1. Baked Apples with Oats and Raisins

This Baked Apples with Oats and Raisins recipe is a delicious and healthy dessert or snack option that perfectly aligns with a gallstone-friendly diet. It's a simple, low-fat, high-fiber meal that's rich in nutrients and natural sweetness. Baked apples provide a good source of fiber, while oats offer additional fiber and complex carbohydrates, which are important for gallbladder health.

INGREDIENTS:

- 4 medium apples (any variety)
- 1/2 cup rolled oats
- 1/4 cup raisins
- 1/4 teaspoon ground cinnamon
- 2 tablespoons maple syrup (optional)

COOKING INSTRUCTIONS:

1. Heat oven to 375°F (190°C).

2. Wash and core the apples, leaving a well in the center of each.

3. In a small bowl, combine the oats, raisins, and cinnamon.

4. Fill the center of each apple with the oat mixture.

5. If you want, sprinkle a small amount of maple syrup over the filling.

6. Place the apples in a baking bowl and add a little water to the bottom of the bowl (about 1/4 inch).

7. Bake for 30-40 minutes, or until the apples are tender when poked with a fork.

8. Serve warm.

PREP TECHNIQUES:

- The apples are baked in the oven until soft.

- Calories: 150-200 kcal

- Protein: 2-3 g

- Fat: 1-2 g

- Carbohydrates: 35-40 g

- Fiber: 5-7 g

Serving Portion: This recipe makes 4 servings.

Cooking Time: 30-40 minutes

Prep Time: 10 minutes

DIET RECIPE NOTE:

This Baked Apples with Oats and Raisins dish is excellent for a gallstone diet since it is low in fat, high in fiber, and devoid of refined grains and added sugars (if you leave out the maple syrup). Apples include soluble fiber, which can help decrease cholesterol and lower the risk of gallstones. Oats give extra fiber and complex carbs, both of which are beneficial to weight management and digestion.

Tip: If you like a sweeter filling, you can add a sprinkle of honey or a sprinkle of brown sugar to the oat mixture. You can also experiment with different spices, such as nutmeg or cardamom, to create your unique taste combinations.

_____

_____

_____

_____

2. Chia Pudding with Mango Puree

This Chia Pudding with Mango Puree recipe is a delicious and nutritious dessert or snack, great for a gallstone-friendly diet. Chia seeds are rich in fiber, which is essential for gallbladder health, and mango gives natural sweetness and vitamins. This recipe is naturally low in fat and cholesterol, making it a guilt-free indulgence.

INGREDIENTS:

- 1/4 cup chia seeds
- 1 cup unsweetened almond milk (or other low-fat milk options)
- 1 ripe mango, peeled and diced
- 1-2 tablespoons honey or maple syrup (optional, adjust to taste)
- Optional toppings: fresh berries, chopped nuts, shredded coconut

COOKING INSTRUCTIONS:

1. In a bowl or jar, combine the chia seeds and almond milk. Stir well to ensure the seeds are evenly distributed.

2. Let the mixture sit for 5 minutes, then stir again to break up any clumps.

3. Cover and refrigerate for at least 2 hours, or preferably overnight, until the chia seeds have absorbed the liquid and formed a pudding-like thickness.

4. While the chia pudding is setting, make the mango puree. In a blender or food processor, puree the diced mango until smooth.

5. Once the chia pudding is ready, layer it with the mango puree in glasses or bowls.

6. Top with your favorite toppings, such as fresh berries, chopped nuts, or shredded coconut.

PREPARATION TECHNIQUES:

- Chia seeds and milk are mixed to combine.
- Mango is pureed in a blender or food processor.
- Chia pudding and mango puree are layered for visual appeal.

NUTRITIONAL VALUES PER SERVING (APPROXIMATE):

- Calories: 200-250 kcal
- Protein: 5-7 g

- Fat: 5-8 g

- Carbohydrates: 30-35 g

- Fiber: 10-12 g

Serving Portion: This recipe makes 2 servings.

Cooking Time: 5 minutes (plus refrigeration time)

Prep Time: 10 minutes

DIET RECIPE NOTE:

This Chia Pudding with Mango Puree is ideal for a gallstone diet. It is naturally low in fat and cholesterol, rich in fiber, and has no processed sugars or artificial additives. Chia seeds and mango contain critical nutrients and help good digestion. However, it is critical to use unsweetened almond milk or other low-fat milk substitutes and avoid adding too many sweets, such as honey or maple syrup.

Tip: For a richer taste, you can use coconut milk instead of almond milk. However, choose a light or reduced-fat variety to keep the fat content in check.

3. Baked Peaches with Honey and Greek Yogurt

This Baked Peaches with Honey and Greek Yogurt recipe gives a delicious and healthy dessert or snack option for individuals on a gallstone diet. Peaches are a low-fat, high-fiber fruit, and Greek yogurt provides protein and probiotics, which can support digestive health. The honey adds natural sweetness, making this meal a satisfying treat without the need for refined sugars or unhealthy fats.

INGREDIENTS:

- 4 ripe peaches, halved and pitted
- 2 tablespoons honey
- 1/2 cup plain, non-fat Greek yogurt
- 1/4 teaspoon ground cinnamon
- Pinch of ground nutmeg (optional)

COOKING INSTRUCTIONS:

1. Heat oven to 375°F (190°C).

2. Place the peach halves cut-side up in a baking bowl.

3. Sprinkle each peach half with 1/2 tablespoon of honey.

4. In a small bowl, combine the Greek yogurt, cinnamon, and nutmeg (if using).

5. Spoon the yogurt mixture evenly over the peaches.

6. Bake for 20-25 minutes, or until the peaches are tender and the yogurt is set.

7. Serve warm or at room temperature.

PREPARATION TECHNIQUES:

- Peaches are halved and the stones are removed.
- Honey is sprinkled over the peaches for sweetness.
- Greek yogurt, cinnamon, and nutmeg are combined to create a topping.
- Peaches are baked until soft and the yogurt is set.

NUTRITIONAL VALUES PER SERVING (APPROXIMATE):

- Calories: 150-200 kcal

- Protein: 8-10 g

- Fat: 0-2 g

- Carbohydrates: 30-35 g

- Fiber: 4-5 g

Serving Portion: This recipe makes 4 servings (one peach half per serving).

Cooking Time: 20-25 minutes

Prep Time: 10 minutes

DIET RECIPE NOTE:

This Baked Peaches with Honey and Greek Yogurt dish is typically suitable for a gallstone diet. Peaches are low in fat and high in fiber, which promotes proper digestion. Greek yogurt contains protein and probiotics, which help improve intestinal health. Individuals with gallstones, on the other hand, should be cautious with the honey part and use it carefully, since excessive sugar consumption might contribute to gallbladder troubles. It is best to speak with a nutritionist to establish the optimum amount of honey for your specific needs and tolerance.

_____

_____

_____

_____

_____

4. Strawberry Sorbet

This Strawberry Sorbet recipe is a refreshing, light, and delicious dessert great for a gallstone-friendly diet. It's naturally sweet, low in fat, and doesn't contain any of the foods you should limit or avoid when managing gallbladder health.

INGREDIENTS:

- 4 cups fresh strawberries, hulled and chopped
- 1/2 cup water
- 1/4 cup honey or maple syrup (optional, adjust to taste)
- 1 tablespoon lemon juice

COOKING INSTRUCTIONS:

1. Combine the strawberries, water, honey/maple syrup (if using), and lemon juice in a blender.

2. Blend until smooth and creamy.

3. Pour the mixture into a freezer-safe container.

4. Freeze for at least 4 hours, or until solid.

5. Before start serving, let the sorbet sit at room temperature for 5-10 minutes to soften slightly.

6. Scoop and enjoy!

PREPARATION TECHNIQUES:

- The key tips are blending all the ingredients until smooth.

NUTRITIONAL VALUES PER SERVING (APPROXIMATE):

- Calories: 100-150 kcal (depending on sweetener used)
- Protein: 1g
- Fat: 0g
- Carbohydrates: 25-35g (depending on the sweetener used)
- Fiber: 3-4g

Serving Portion: This recipe makes about 4 servings.

Cooking Time: 5 minutes (active) + 4 hours (freezing)

Prep Time: 10 minutes

DIET RECIPE NOTE:

This strawberry sorbet is an excellent choice for a gallstone diet. It's naturally sweet from the fruit, low in fat, and cholesterol-free. Be aware of the amount of honey or maple syrup you use, since too much sugar can be harmful to gallbladder health.

Tips:

- Use ripe strawberries for the best taste.

- If you don't have fresh strawberries, you can use frozen strawberries. Just thaw them slightly before blending.

- For a smoother texture, strain the mixture through a fine-mesh sieve before freezing.

- Feel free to experiment with other fruits like raspberries, blueberries, or mangoes.

- For a more sophisticated taste, add a few leaves of fresh mint or basil to the blender.

_____

_____

_____

_____

_____

5. Baked Apples with Cinnamon

Baked apples with cinnamon give a warm, comforting, and naturally sweet dessert that aligns greatly with a gallstone-friendly diet. Apples are a good source of fiber, which helps promote healthy digestion and can reduce the risk of gallstones. The addition of cinnamon not only adds a delicious taste but may also offer anti-inflammatory benefits.

INGREDIENTS:

- 4 medium apples (choose varieties like Honeycrisp, Fuji, or Granny Smith)

- 1/4 cup water

- 1 tablespoon lemon juice

- 2 teaspoons ground cinnamon

- 1/4 teaspoon ground nutmeg (optional)

COOKING INSTRUCTIONS:

1. Heat oven to 375°F (190°C).

2. Wash and core the apples, leaving the bottom intact.

3. Place the apples in a baking bowl and pour the water and lemon juice into the bottom of the bowl.

4. In a small bowl, combine the cinnamon and nutmeg (if using).

5. Sprinkle the cinnamon mixture evenly over the tops of the apples.

6. Bake for 30-40 minutes, or until the apples are soft when pierced with a fork.

7. Serve warm.

PREPARATION TECHNIQUES:

- Apples are cored to remove the seeds and create a hollow center for filling.

- Apples are baked in the oven until soft.

NUTRITIONAL VALUES PER SERVING (APPROXIMATE):

- Calories: 100-120 kcal

- Protein: 0-1 g

- Fat: 0-1 g

- Carbohydrates: 25-30 g

- Fiber: 4-5 g

Serving Portion: This recipe makes 4 servings.

Cooking Time: 30-40 minutes

Prep Time: 10 minutes

DIET RECIPE NOTE:

This Baked Apples with Cinnamon dish is ideal for a gallstone diet. It's low in fat, high in fiber, and has no added sugars or processed grains. Apples are high in soluble fiber, which can decrease cholesterol and reduce the incidence of gallstones. Cinnamon may provide extra advantages for gallbladder health. This easy and tasty dish will satisfy your sweet appetite while helping you meet your nutritional objectives.

Tips:

- You can add a sprinkle of chopped nuts, such as walnuts or pecans, for added crunch and protein.
- For a vegan option, you can replace the butter with a plant-based butter option.
- If you like a sweeter dessert, you can sprinkle a small amount of maple syrup or honey over the apples before baking.

6. Pineapple and Cottage Cheese

This Pineapple and Cottage Cheese Parfait is a light, refreshing, and nutritious snack or dessert great for a gallstone-friendly diet. Pineapple is rich in fiber and bromelain, an enzyme that aids digestion, while cottage cheese is a low-fat protein source. This combination offers a delicious balance of sweetness and tanginess while supporting gallbladder health.

INGREDIENTS:

- 1 cup fresh pineapple chunks
- 1/2 cup low-fat or fat-free cottage cheese
- 1 tablespoon chopped walnuts or almonds (optional)
- 1/4 teaspoon cinnamon (optional)

COOKING INSTRUCTIONS:

1. If using fresh pineapple, cut it into bite-sized chunks.

2. In a small bowl or glass, layer the pineapple and cottage cheese. You can create multiple layers for a visually appealing parfait.

3. Sprinkle with chopped nuts and cinnamon, if you want.

4. Enjoy immediately or chill for later.

PREPARATION TECHNIQUES:

- Pineapple is chopped into bite-sized pieces.
- Ingredients are layered in a bowl or glass to create a parfait.

NUTRITIONAL VALUES PER SERVING (APPROXIMATE):

- Calories: 150-200 kcal
- Protein: 10-15 g
- Fat: 5-8 g
- Carbohydrates: 15-20 g
- Fiber: 2-3 g

Serving Portion: This recipe makes 1 serving.

Cooking Time: 5 minutes

Prep Time: 5 minutes

This Pineapple and Cottage Cheese Parfait is appropriate for the gallstone diet. It is low in fat, high in protein and fiber, and does not contain any of the items that should be limited or avoided on a gallstone diet. The pineapple contains vitamins and minerals, and the cottage cheese contains lean protein. The nuts and cinnamon provide taste and extra nutrients without causing problems with the gallbladder.

Tip: If you like a smoother texture, you can blend the cottage cheese with a little bit of milk or yogurt before layering.

_____

_____

_____

_____

_____

7. Raspberry and Lemon Gelatin

This Raspberry and Lemon Gelatin recipe is a light, refreshing, and delicious dessert that great for satisfying your sweet tooth while adhering to a gallstone-friendly diet. It avoids high-fat dairy and refined sugars, making it a guilt-free treat that supports gallbladder health.

INGREDIENTS:

- 1 cup fresh or frozen raspberries
- 1/4 cup freshly squeezed lemon juice
- 1/4 cup honey or maple syrup (adjust to taste)
- 4 packets of unflavored gelatin powder
- 2 cups water

COOKING INSTRUCTIONS:

1. In a saucepan, combine the raspberries, lemon juice, and honey or maple syrup. Heat over medium heat, stirring occasionally, until the raspberries are softened and the mixture is heated through.

2. In a separate bowl, sprinkle the gelatin powder over 1/2 cup of cold water. Let it sit for a few minutes to bloom.

3. Add the remaining 1.5 cups of water to the saucepan with the raspberry mixture. Bring to a cook, then remove from heat.

4. Add the bloomed gelatin to the warm raspberry mixture and stir until the gelatin is completely dissolved.

5. Strain the mixture through a fine-mesh sieve to remove any seeds or pulp.

6. Pour the mixture into individual serving meals or molds.

7. Refrigerate for at least 4 hours, or until the gelatin is set.

PREPARATION TECHNIQUES:

- The raspberries and lemon juice are heated to release their taste and create a base for the gelatin.
- The gelatin is bloomed in cold water to ensure smooth dissolution.
- The mixture is cooked to incorporate the gelatin and dissolve it completely.

- The mixture is strained to remove any seeds or pulp for a smooth texture.

- The gelatin is set in the refrigerator until firm.

- Calories: 80-100 kcal (depending on sweetener used)

- Protein: 2-3 g

- Fat: 0 g

- Carbohydrates: 20-25 g

- Fiber: 1-2 g

Serving Portion: This recipe makes 4-6 servings.

Cooking Time: 15 minutes

Prep Time: 10 minutes

DIET RECIPE NOTE:

This Raspberry and Lemon Gelatin dish is ideal for a gallstone diet since it is low in fat, contains no processed sugars, and incorporates fresh fruit for sweetness and taste. It avoids all of the items that should be limited or avoided on a gallstone diet. However, be aware of the amount of honey or maple syrup used, since too much sugar can still be harmful to gallbladder health. Adjust the sweetness to suit your taste and dietary requirements.

_____

_____

_____

_____

_____

8. Pear and Almond Crumble

This Pear and Almond Crumble recipe is a delicious and healthy dessert option that is greatly suitable for a gallstone-friendly diet. It has the natural sweetness of pears, the heart-healthy fats of almonds, and the wholesome goodness of whole-grain oats. This crumble is not only delicious but also easy to digest, making it a guilt-free indulgence for those managing gallbladder health.

INGREDIENTS:

FILLING:

- 4 ripe pears, peeled, cored, and chopped
- 1 tablespoon lemon juice
- 1/4 cup water
- 1/4 teaspoon ground cinnamon

CRUMBLE TOPPING:

- 1/2 cup rolled oats
- 1/4 cup almond flour
- 1/4 cup chopped almonds
- 2 tablespoons maple syrup or honey
- 1 tablespoon coconut oil, melted

COOKING INSTRUCTIONS:

1. Heat oven to 375°F (190°C).

2. In a medium saucepan, combine the chopped pears, lemon juice, water, and cinnamon. Cook over medium heat until the pears are softened, about 10 minutes.

3. Transfer the cooked pears to a baking bowl.

4. In a separate bowl, combine the rolled oats, almond flour, chopped almonds, maple syrup (or honey), and melted coconut oil. Mix well until crumbly.

5. Sprinkle the crumble topping evenly over the pears in the baking bowl.

6. Bake for 20-25 minutes, or until the topping is golden brown and the pears are bubbly.

7. Let cool slightly before serving.

- Pears are chopped into bite-sized pieces.

- Pears are simmered in a saucepan until softened.

- Crumble topping ingredients are mixed.

- Crumble is baked in the oven until golden brown.

NUTRITIONAL VALUES PER SERVING (APPROXIMATE):

- Calories: 250-300 kcal

- Protein: 5-7 g

- Fat: 15-20 g (mostly healthy fats from almonds and coconut oil)

- Carbohydrates: 25-30 g

- Fiber: 5-7 g

Serving Portion: This recipe makes 4-6 servings.

Cooking Time: 20-25 minutes

Prep Time: 15 minutes

DIET RECIPE NOTE:

This Pear and Almond Crumble is ideal for a gallstone diet. It is naturally sweet, low in saturated fat, and high in fiber, all of which can help regulate bile production and prevent gallstones from forming. It also avoids all of the items that should be limited or avoided on a gallstone diet.

Tips:

- You can use other fruits like apples or berries instead of pears.

- Feel free to add a pinch of nutmeg or ginger to the filling for additional flavor.

- For a vegan version, use agave nectar instead of honey and vegan butter instead of coconut oil.

- Serve warm with a dollop of low-fat Greek yogurt or a drizzle of almond milk.

9. Apricot and Yogurt Parfait

This Apricot and Yogurt Parfait is a light, refreshing, and nutritious breakfast or snack option that aligns greatly with a gallstone-friendly diet. It combines the natural sweetness of apricots with the creamy goodness of yogurt and the crunch of granola, providing a tasty and balanced meal.

INGREDIENTS:

- 1 cup plain non-fat Greek yogurt
- 2-3 fresh apricots, pitted and diced (or 1/2 cup canned apricots in their juice, drained)
- 1/4 cup low-fat granola
- 1 tablespoon honey (optional, for added sweetness)

COOKING INSTRUCTIONS:

1. In a glass or bowl, layer half of the yogurt, followed by half of the diced apricots, and half of the granola.

2. Repeat the layers with the remaining yogurt, apricots, and granola.

3. Sprinkle with honey, if desired.

4. Enjoy immediately or refrigerate for later.

PREPARATION TECHNIQUES:

- Apricots are chopped or diced into bite-sized pieces.
- Ingredients are layered in a glass or bowl for visual appeal and balanced taste.

Nutritional Values Per Serving (approximate):

- Calories: 200-250 kcal
- Protein: 10-12 g
- Fat: 2-4 g
- Carbohydrates: 30-35 g
- Fiber: 4-5 g

Serving Portion: This recipe makes one serving.

Cooking Time: 5 minutes

Prep Time: 5 minutes

This Apricot and Yogurt Parfait is ideal for a gallstone diet. It is low in fat, high in protein and fiber, and does not contain any of the items that should be limited or avoided on a gallstone diet. Apricots give natural sweetness and fiber, yogurt contains protein and bacteria for digestive health, and granola provides a pleasant crunch. To limit your fat intake, use low-fat granola.

Tips:

- You can use any type of fruit you prefer, such as berries, peaches, or plums.

- To increase the fiber content, add a tablespoon of chia seeds or ground flaxseeds to the yogurt.

- If you're using canned apricots, be sure to choose those rich in their juice, not in heavy syrup.

- For a vegan option, use plant-based yogurt and substitute maple syrup or agave nectar for honey.

10. Berries Gazpacho

This refreshing Berries Gazpacho is a delicious twist on the classic Spanish chilled soup. It's bursting with the sweetness of berries, the coolness of cucumber, and the tangy zest of citrus. This recipe is a great choice for a gallstone-friendly diet as it's low in fat, high in fiber, and packed with vitamins and antioxidants.

INGREDIENTS:

- 2 cups mixed berries (strawberries, blueberries, raspberries, blackberries)
- 1 cucumber, peeled and chopped
- 1/2 red bell pepper, chopped
- 1/4 red onion, chopped
- 2 tablespoons red wine vinegar
- 1 tablespoon olive oil
- 1/4 cup chopped fresh mint
- Salt and pepper to taste

COOKING INSTRUCTIONS:

1. Combine all ingredients in a blender or food processor.

2. Blend until smooth, adding water if needed to reach desired thickness.

3. Season with salt and pepper to taste.

4. Chill in the refrigerator for at least 2 hours before serving.

PREPARATION TECHNIQUES:

- The vegetables and mint are finely chopped for a smooth gazpacho consistency.
- All ingredients are blended until smooth.
- Gazpacho is chilled to help its refreshing qualities.

NUTRITIONAL VALUES PER SERVING (APPROXIMATE):

- Calories: 100-150 kcal
- Protein: 2-3 g
- Fat: 5-8 g
- Carbohydrates: 15-20 g

- Fiber: 4-6 g

Serving Portion: This recipe makes 4 servings.

Cooking Time: 10 minutes (blending time)

Prep Time: 15 minutes

DIET RECIPE NOTE:

This Berries Gazpacho dish is ideal for a gallstone diet. It is naturally low in fat and cholesterol, with plenty of fiber from the berries and veggies. It also excludes all of the things that are advised to be limited or avoided on a gallstone diet, including fried meals, fatty meats, full-fat dairy, refined cereals, and sweetened drinks.

Tips:

- Feel free to adjust the amount of red onion or vinegar to suit your taste preferences.
- For a spicier version, add a pinch of cayenne pepper or a small jalapeno pepper (seeds removed).
- Garnish with additional fresh berries or mint leaves before serving.
- This gazpacho can be stored in the refrigerator for up to 3 days.

_____

_____

_____

_____

_____

11. Beans & Cauliflower Hummus

This Beans & Cauliflower Hummus recipe is a delicious and nutritious option to traditional hummus, making it a great choice for a gallstone-friendly diet. It combines the creamy texture of beans with the light and fiber-rich cauliflower, resulting in a satisfying dip or spread.

INGREDIENTS:

- 1 head cauliflower, cut into florets
- 1 can (15 ounces) cannellini beans, drained and rinsed
- 2 tablespoons tahini
- 2 tablespoons lemon juice
- 2 cloves garlic, minced
- 1/4 cup olive oil
- Salt and pepper to taste
- Optional toppings: chopped fresh herbs (parsley, cilantro), paprika, olive oil sprinkle

COOKING INSTRUCTIONS:

1. Steam or roast the cauliflower florets until soft.

2. In a food processor, combine the cooked cauliflower, cannellini beans, tahini, lemon juice, garlic, and olive oil.

3. Process until smooth and creamy, scraping down the sides as needed.

4. Season with salt and pepper to taste.

5. Transfer to a serving bowl and top with desired toppings.

PREPARATION TECHNIQUES:

- Cauliflower is cooked until soft.
- Ingredients are blended in a food processor until smooth.

NUTRITIONAL VALUES PER SERVING (APPROXIMATE):

- Calories: 150-200 kcal
- Protein: 5-7 g
- Fat: 10-15 g

- Carbohydrates: 10-15 g

- Fiber: 5-7 g

Serving Portion: This recipe yields approximately 2 cups of hummus.

Cooking Time: 15-20 minutes (excluding cauliflower cooking time)

Prep Time: 10 minutes

DIET RECIPE NOTE:

This Beans and Cauliflower Hummus is typically appropriate for a gallstone diet. It is low in saturated fat, high in fiber, and does not contain any of the items that should be limited or avoided on a gallstone diet. However, tahini is heavy in fat, so use it sparingly. If you are very sensitive to fats, consider using less tahini or olive oil.

Tips:

- For a smoother texture, remove the skins from the cannellini beans before processing.

- Adjust the number of garlic and lemon juice to your liking.

- Serve with whole-wheat pita bread, vegetables, or crackers for dipping.

- Leftover hummus can be stored in an airtight bowl in the refrigerator for up to 5 days.

12. Black Beans Dip

This Black Bean Dip recipe is a delicious, healthy, and satisfying appetizer or snack great for a gallstone-friendly diet. Black beans are a great source of fiber and protein, both of which are beneficial for gallbladder health. This recipe avoids high-fat ingredients like sour cream and cheese, making it a lighter and healthier option.

INGREDIENTS:

- 1 (15-ounce) can black beans, rinsed and drained
- 1/4 cup salsa (mild or medium heat)
- 2 cloves garlic, minced
- 1 tablespoon lime juice
- 1/4 teaspoon ground cumin
- Pinch of salt
- 1/4 cup chopped fresh cilantro (optional)

COOKING INSTRUCTIONS:

1. In a food processor or blender, combine all ingredients except cilantro.

2. Process until smooth and creamy, scraping down the sides as needed.

3. If the dip is too thick, add a tablespoon or two of water to reach the desired thickness.

4. Stir in the chopped cilantro if using.

5. Serve with whole-wheat pita bread, chopped vegetables, or baked tortilla chips.

PREPARATION TECHNIQUES:

- Canned black beans are drained and rinsed to remove excess sodium.
- Garlic is minced for even distribution of taste.
- All ingredients are blended until smooth and creamy.

NUTRITIONAL VALUES PER SERVING (APPROXIMATE):

- Calories: 100-120 kcal
- Protein: 5-7 g

- Fat: 1-2 g

- Carbohydrates: 15-20 g

- Fiber: 6-8 g

Serving Portion: This recipe makes about 1.5 cups of dip.

Cooking Time: 5 minutes

Prep Time: 5 minutes

DIET RECIPE NOTE:

This Black Bean Dip dish is suitable for a gallstone diet. It is low in fat, high in fiber, and does not contain any of the items that should be limited or avoided on a gallstone diet. Black beans provide protein and fiber, both of which are beneficial to gallbladder health. The salsa, garlic, lime juice, and cumin provide a taste without the use of bad fats or dairy ingredients.

Tips:

- For a spicier dip, add a pinch of cayenne pepper or a chopped jalapeño pepper.

- To make this recipe ahead of time, prepare the dip and store it in the refrigerator for up to 3 days.

- For a variety, you can add other ingredients like roasted corn, chopped red onion, or diced avocado.

13.   Corn & Beans Relish

This Corn & Beans Relish is a bright and delicious meal that's perfect for those on a gallstone diet. It's rich in fiber-rich vegetables, and lean protein from the beans, and avoids high-fat ingredients like mayonnaise or cheese often found in traditional relishes. This recipe is a delicious way to add zest and color to your meals while supporting your gallbladder health.

INGREDIENTS:

- 1 (15-ounce) can black beans, rinsed and drained
- 1 (15-ounce) can of corn, drained
- 1/2 red bell pepper, diced
- 1/2 green bell pepper, diced
- 1/4 cup red onion, diced
- 1/4 cup chopped fresh cilantro
- 2 tablespoons lime juice
- 1 tablespoon olive oil
- 1/2 teaspoon cumin
- 1/4 teaspoon chili powder
- Salt and pepper to taste

COOKING INSTRUCTIONS:

1. In a large bowl, combine the black beans, corn, red bell pepper, green bell pepper, red onion, and cilantro.

2. In a separate small bowl, mix the lime juice, olive oil, cumin, chili powder, salt, and pepper.

3. Pour the dressing over the bean and corn mixture and stir to combine.

4. Refrigerate for at least 30 minutes to allow the taste to meld.

5. Serve chilled as a side bowl or topping for grilled chicken or fish.

PREPARATION TECHNIQUES:

- Vegetables are chopped into small, uniform pieces.
- Ingredients are combined in a bowl.

- Dressing ingredients are mixed until emulsified.

- Calories: 150-200 kcal

- Protein: 8-10 g

- Fat: 5-7 g

- Carbohydrates: 20-25 g

- Fiber: 6-8 g

Serving Portion: This recipe makes 4-6 servings.

Cooking Time: 15 minutes (mostly inactive chilling time)

Prep Time: 15 minutes

DIET RECIPE NOTE:

This Corn & Beans Relish is great for a gallstone diet since it is strong in fiber and low in fat. It eliminates all of the items that should be limited on a gallstone diet, making it a safe and healthful option. Beans and maize offer important nutrients, while vegetables and herbs add freshness and taste. Feel free to alter the spice level to your liking.

---

14. Chickpeas & Carrot Hummus

This Chickpeas & Carrot Hummus recipe is a delicious and nutritious option to traditional hummus, making it a great choice for a gallstone-friendly diet. It is rich in fiber from chickpeas and carrots, which can help regulate digestion and promote gallbladder health. Additionally, it is naturally low in fat and cholesterol, making it a safe and satisfying snack or appetizer.

INGREDIENTS:

- 1 can (15 ounces) chickpeas, drained and rinsed
- 1 cup cooked carrots, roughly chopped
- 1/4 cup tahini
- 1/4 cup lemon juice
- 1 garlic clove, minced
- 1/4 cup extra virgin olive oil
- Salt and pepper to taste
- Optional toppings: chopped fresh parsley, paprika, a drizzle of olive oil

COOKING INSTRUCTIONS:

1. In a food processor, combine the chickpeas, carrots, tahini, lemon juice, and garlic.

2. Process until smooth, stopping to scrape down the sides as needed.

3. With the food processor running, slowly sprinkle in the olive oil until the desired thickness is reached.

4. Season with salt and pepper to taste.

5. Transfer to a serving bowl and garnish with optional toppings.

PREPARATION TECHNIQUES:

- Chickpeas are drained and rinsed to remove excess sodium and starch.
- Carrots are roughly chopped for easier blending.
- All ingredients are pureed in a food processor until smooth.

NUTRITIONAL VALUES PER SERVING (APPROXIMATE):

- Calories: 150-200 kcal (depending on serving size and toppings)

- Protein: 5-7 g

- Fat: 8-12 g (mostly healthy unsaturated fats)

- Carbohydrates: 15-20 g

- Fiber: 6-8 g

Serving Portion: This recipe yields approximately 2 cups of hummus

Cooking Time: 10 minutes (mostly hands-off while the food processor runs)

Prep Time: 10 minutes

DIET RECIPE NOTE:

This Chickpeas & Carrot Hummus dish is perfect for a gallstone diet since it eliminates all of the items that should be limited or avoided. It is naturally low in fat and cholesterol, rich in fiber, and has no added sugars. Chickpeas and carrots are high in protein and complex carbs, both of which can aid with digestion and gallbladder function.

Tip: To increase the fiber content of this recipe further, you can leave the skins on the carrots before cooking them.

Self-Reflection Questions:

1. What are my typical snack and dessert choices, and how well do they align with a gallstone-friendly diet?

_____

_____

_____

_____

2. Am I willing to explore new and healthier snack and dessert options to support my gallbladder health?

_____

_____

_____

_____

_____

3. What are my liking for snack and dessert flavors and textures, and how can I incorporate them into gallstone-friendly treats?

_____

_____

_____

_____

4. What are my triggers for unhealthy snacking or overindulging in desserts? How can I manage these triggers to stay on track with my dietary goals?

_____

_____

_____

_____

5. How can I make sure I have healthy and satisfying snack and dessert options readily available to avoid reaching for unhealthy choices?

_____

_____

_____

CHAPTER 8:

GALLSTONE-FRIENDLY VEGETARIAN & VEGAN DIET

1. Roasted Vegetable Quinoa Bowl

This Roasted Vegetable Quinoa Bowl is a bright, delicious, and nutritious meal great for a gallstone-friendly diet. It is rich in fiber-rich vegetables and protein-rich quinoa, which promote healthy digestion and support gallbladder function. Roasting the vegetables brings out their natural sweetness and enhances their flavor without the need for added fats or oils.

INGREDIENTS:

- 1 cup quinoa

- 2 cups water

- 1 tablespoon olive oil

- 1 sweet potato, diced

- 1 red bell pepper, diced

- 1 zucchini, diced

- 1/2 red onion, diced

- 1 teaspoon dried oregano

- 1/2 teaspoon salt

- 1/4 teaspoon black pepper

- Optional toppings: chopped fresh herbs (parsley, cilantro), a drizzle of balsamic glaze

COOKING INSTRUCTIONS:

1. Heat oven to 400°F (200°C).

2. Rinse the quinoa thoroughly. Combine it with water in a saucepan. Bring to a boil, then reduce heat to low, cover, and cook for 15 minutes or until the quinoa is cooked.

3. While the quinoa is cooking, toss the diced vegetables with olive oil, oregano, salt, and pepper in a large bowl.

4. Spread the vegetables in a single layer on a baking sheet. Roast for 20-25 minutes, or until tender and slightly browned.

5. Once the quinoa is cooked, fluff it with a fork.

6. Divide the quinoa among bowls and top with the roasted vegetables.

7. Garnish with optional toppings and serve warm.

COOKING TECHNIQUES:

- Vegetables are roasted in the oven for a healthy cooking method.

- Quinoa is cooked in water until cooked.

- Vegetables are tossed with oil and seasonings for even coating.

NUTRITIONAL VALUES PER SERVING (APPROXIMATE):

- Calories: 350-400 kcal

- Protein: 10-12 g

- Fat: 10-15 g

- Carbohydrates: 50-60 g

- Fiber: 10-12 g

Serving Portion: This recipe makes 4 servings.

Cooking Time: 35-40 minutes

Prep Time: 15 minutes

DIET RECIPE NOTE:

This Roasted Vegetable Quinoa Bowl is ideal for a gallstone diet. It is low in fat, high in fiber, and does not contain any of the items that are restricted or avoided on this diet. Quinoa is high in protein and complex carbs, while roasted veggies are rich in vitamins, minerals, and antioxidants. This recipe is naturally low in salt and cholesterol, making it a heart-healthy choice.

Tip: is good you select this recipe with your favorite vegetables. Other good options include broccoli, cauliflower, Brussels sprouts, or carrots. You can also add a sprinkle of balsamic glaze for more taste.

2. Vegetable Stir-Fry with Brown Rice

This Vegetable Stir-Fry with Brown Rice recipe is a nutritious and delicious meal that aligns perfectly with a gallstone-friendly diet. It is rich in fiber-rich vegetables and whole grains, which promote healthy digestion and gallbladder function. The stir-frying technique uses minimal oil, ensuring the meal remains low in fat. It is a versatile recipe, allowing you to select the vegetables based on your liking and seasonal availability.

INGREDIENTS:

- 1 cup brown rice, cooked
- 1 tablespoon olive oil
- 1 onion, chopped
- 2 cloves garlic, minced
- 1 bell pepper (any color), sliced
- 1 cup broccoli florets
- 1/2 cup sliced carrots
- 1/2 cup snow peas or snap peas
- 2 tablespoons low-sodium soy sauce (or tamari for gluten-free)
- 1 tablespoon rice vinegar
- 1/4 teaspoon ground ginger
- Salt and pepper to taste

COOKING INSTRUCTIONS:

1. Cook the brown rice according to package instructions.

2. While the rice is cooking, heat the olive oil in a large pan or wok over medium-high heat.

3. Add the onion and garlic and cook until softened about 2 minutes.

4. Add the bell pepper, broccoli, carrots, and snow peas (or snap peas) to the pan. Stir-fry for 5-7 minutes, or until the vegetables are soft-crisp.

5. Add the cooked rice, soy sauce (or tamari), rice vinegar, and ginger to the pan. Stir-fry for another 2-3 minutes, or until heated through.

6. Season with salt and pepper to taste.   7. Serve hot.

COOKING TECHNIQUES:

- Vegetables and rice are stir-fried in a small quantity of oil over high heat for a quick and healthy cooking method.

NUTRITIONAL VALUES PER SERVING (APPROXIMATE):

- Calories: 300-350 kcal

- Protein: 10-12 g

- Fat: 5-8 g

- Carbohydrates: 50-55 g

- Fiber: 6-8 g

Serving Portion: This recipe makes 4 servings.

Cooking Time: 25-30 minutes

Prep Time: 15 minutes

DIET RECIPE NOTE:

This Vegetable Stir-Fry with Brown Rice dish is ideal for a gallstone diet. It avoids all of the foods you need to restrict or avoid on this diet and is high in nutrients that promote gallbladder health. Brown rice is a complete grain that contains fiber, which aids in digestion and may lower the risk of gallstones. A variety of veggies provides vitamins, minerals, and antioxidants, while stir-frying reduces fat content.

Tip: is good to select this recipe with your favorite vegetables. You can add mushrooms, zucchini, asparagus, or any other non-starchy vegetables you prefer.

3. Sweet Potato Black Bean Burgers

These Sweet Potato Black Bean Burgers are a delicious, nutritious, and satisfying option to local beef burgers. They are rich in fiber, protein, and vital nutrients, making them a great option for a gallstone-friendly diet. The sweet potatoes provide complex carbohydrates and vitamins, while the black beans offer a good source of protein and fiber.

INGREDIENTS:

- 1 large sweet potato, baked or steamed
- 1 can (15 ounces) black beans, rinsed and drained
- 1/2 cup rolled oats
- 1/4 cup chopped onion
- 1/4 cup chopped red bell pepper
- 1 tablespoon chili powder
- 1 teaspoon cumin
- 1/2 teaspoon garlic powder
- Salt and pepper to taste

COOKING INSTRUCTIONS:

1. Heat oven to 375°F (190°C). Line a baking sheet with parchment paper.

2. In a large bowl, mash the sweet potato.

3. Add the black beans, oats, onion, bell pepper, chili powder, cumin, garlic powder, salt, and pepper. Mix well to combine.

4. Form the mixture into 4-6 patties.

5. Place the patties on the prepared baking sheet and bake for 20-25 minutes, or until golden brown and firm.

COOKING TECHNIQUES:

- The patties are baked in the oven for a healthy cooking method.
- The sweet potato and black beans are mashed to create a cohesive mixture.

NUTRITIONAL VALUES PER SERVING (APPROXIMATE):

- Calories: 200-250 kcal
- Protein: 10-12 g

- Fat: 5-8 g (mostly healthy unsaturated fats)

- Carbohydrates: 30-35 g

- Fiber: 8-10 g

Serving Portion: This recipe makes 4-6 patties.

Cooking Time: 20-25 minutes

Prep Time: 15 minutes

DIET RECIPE NOTE:

These Sweet Potato Black Bean Burgers are acceptable for a gallstone diet since they do not contain any of the items that should be limited or avoided. They're low in fat, high in fiber, and loaded with nutrients. Sweet potatoes and black beans are rich in complex carbs and protein, which can help regulate digestion and improve gallbladder function.

Tip: Serve these burgers on whole-wheat buns or lettuce wraps for a more boost of fiber. Top with your favorite vegetables, avocado, or a dollop of plain Greek yogurt for added taste and nutrition.

_____

_____

_____

_____

4. Veggie Lentil Soup

This Veggie Lentil Soup is a hearty, delicious, and nutritious meal that aligns perfectly with a gallstone-friendly diet. Lentils are a great source of protein and fiber, promoting healthy digestion and gallbladder function. The abundance of vegetables provides essential vitamins, minerals, and antioxidants. This soup is low in fat and cholesterol, making it a comforting and satisfying meal for those managing gallstones.

INGREDIENTS:

- 1 tablespoon olive oil
- 1 onion, chopped
- 2 carrots, chopped
- 2 celery stalks, chopped
- 4 cloves garlic, minced
- 1 teaspoon dried oregano
- 1/2 teaspoon dried thyme
- 6 cups vegetable broth
- 1 cup red lentils, rinsed
- 1 (14.5-ounce) can of diced tomatoes, undrained
- 1 cup chopped kale or spinach
- Salt and pepper to taste

COOKING INSTRUCTIONS:

1. Heat the olive oil in a large pot over medium heat. Add the onion, carrots, and celery and cook until softened, about 5 minutes.

2. Add the garlic, oregano, and thyme and cook for 1 minute more.

3. Pour in the vegetable broth and add the lentils and diced tomatoes. Bring to a boil, then reduce heat and cook for 20-25 minutes, or until the lentils are soft.

4. Stir in the kale or spinach and cook for an additional 2-3 minutes, or until wilted.

5. Season with salt and pepper to taste. Serve hot.

COOKING TECHNIQUES:

- Vegetables are sautéed in olive oil to help their taste.

- Lentils are cooked in broth until soft.

- Kale or spinach is added at the end and wilted into the soup.

NUTRITIONAL VALUES PER SERVING (APPROXIMATE):

- Calories: 250-300 kcal

- Protein: 15-20 g

- Fat: 5-8 g

- Carbohydrates: 35-40 g

- Fiber: 15-20 g

Serving Portion: This recipe makes 6-8 servings.

Cooking Time: 30-35 minutes

Prep Time: 15 minutes

DIET RECIPE NOTE:

This Veggie Lentil Soup is perfect for those on a gallstone diet. It's low in fat and cholesterol, high in fiber, and full of minerals. Lentils are rich in plant-based protein and fiber, while veggies include vital vitamins and minerals. This soup reduces all of the foods that should be limited or avoided on a gallstone diet, making it a safe and nutritious choice.

Tip: For more taste, you can add a bay leaf to the soup while it cooks and remove it before serving. You can also garnish the soup with a sprinkle of fresh herbs or a dollop of plain yogurt.

5. Mediterranean Quinoa Salad

This Mediterranean Quinoa Salad is a refreshing and nutritious meal, perfect for a gallstone-friendly diet. It's rich in fiber-rich vegetables, lean protein from chickpeas, and heart-healthy fats from olive oil and olives. The spicy textures make it a satisfying and delicious meal that supports gallbladder health.

INGREDIENTS:

- 1 cup quinoa, cooked and cooled
- 1 cucumber, diced
- 1 bell pepper (any color), diced
- 1/2 cup cherry tomatoes, halved
- 1/2 cup Kalamata olives, pitted and halved
- 1/2 cup crumbled feta cheese (optional)
- 1/4 cup chopped fresh parsley
- 1/4 cup chopped fresh mint
- 1 can (15 ounces) chickpeas, drained and rinsed

FOR THE DRESSING:

- 1/4 cup olive oil
- 2 tablespoons lemon juice
- 1 tablespoon red wine vinegar
- 1 teaspoon Dijon mustard
- 1/2 teaspoon dried oregano
- Salt and pepper to taste

COOKING INSTRUCTIONS:

1. In a large bowl, combine the cooked quinoa, cucumber, bell pepper, cherry tomatoes, olives, feta cheese (if using), parsley, mint, and chickpeas.

2. In a separate small bowl, mix the olive oil, lemon juice, red wine vinegar, Dijon mustard, oregano, salt, and pepper.

3. Pour the dressing over the salad and toss to combine.

4. Serve chilled or at room temperature.

- Quinoa is cooked according to package instructions.

- Vegetables and herbs are chopped into bite-sized pieces.

- Dressing ingredients are mixed until emulsified.

- Salad ingredients and dressing are tossed together to combine.

NUTRITIONAL VALUES PER SERVING (APPROXIMATE):

- Calories: 350-400 kcal

- Protein: 15-20 g

- Fat: 15-20 g (mostly healthy unsaturated fats)

- Carbohydrates: 35-40 g

- Fiber: 10-12 g

Serving Portion: This recipe makes 4-6 servings.

Cooking Time: 20 minutes (plus additional time for quinoa to cook and cool)

Prep Time: 15 minutes

DIET RECIPE NOTE:

This Mediterranean Quinoa Salad is suitable for a gallstone diet. It is low in fat, high in fiber, and does not contain any of the products that are restricted or avoided on this diet. Quinoa and chickpeas are high in protein and complex carbs, while veggies and herbs include vitamins, minerals, and antioxidants. Olive oil and olives are high in good fats, which help improve gallbladder health.

Tip: To increase the protein content of this salad, you can add grilled chicken or fish.

6. Spinach and Mushroom Stuffed Portobello Mushrooms

his Spinach and Mushroom Stuffed Portobello Mushrooms recipe is a delicious and nutritious vegetarian meal that's perfect for those following a gallstone-friendly diet. Portobello mushrooms are rich in nutrients and fiber, while the spinach and mushroom filling provide a good source of protein and vitamins. This meal is baked instead of fried, making it a healthier option for many stuffed mushroom recipes.

INGREDIENTS:

- 4 large portobello mushroom caps, stems, and gills removed
- 1 tablespoon olive oil
- 1/2 cup chopped onion
- 1/2 cup chopped cremini mushrooms
- 2 cloves garlic, minced
- 4 cups fresh baby spinach
- 1/4 cup grated Parmesan cheese (optional)
- Salt and pepper to taste

COOKING INSTRUCTIONS:

1. Heat oven to 400°F (200°C).

2. Brush both sides of the portobello caps with olive oil and season with salt and pepper.

3. Place the mushroom caps, gill-side up, on a baking sheet.

4. Bake for 10 minutes.

5. While the mushrooms are baking, heat the olive oil in a pan over medium heat. Add the onion and cook until softened about 5 minutes.

6. Add the cremini mushrooms and cook until browned, about 5 minutes more.

7. Stir in the garlic and cook for 30 seconds.

8. Add the spinach and cook until wilted, about 2 minutes.

9. Remove the mushroom caps from the oven and fill each with the spinach and mushroom mixture.

10. Sprinkle with Parmesan cheese (if using).

11. Bake for an additional 10-15 minutes, or
    until the mushrooms are tender and the
    filling is heated through.

COOKING TECHNIQUES:

- Portobello mushrooms are baked for a healthy cooking method.

- Onion, mushrooms, and garlic are sautéed to help taste.

- Spinach is cooked until wilted.

- The cooked vegetables are used to stuff the mushroom caps.

NUTRITIONAL VALUES PER SERVING (APPROXIMATE):

- Calories: 200-250 kcal

- Protein: 10-12 g

- Fat: 10-15 g (mostly healthy unsaturated fats from olive oil)

- Carbohydrates: 15-20 g

- Fiber: 5-7 g

Serving Portion: This recipe makes 4 servings.

Cooking Time: 25-30 minutes

Prep Time: 15 minutes

DIET RECIPE NOTE:

This Spinach and Mushroom Stuffed Portobello Mushrooms dish is appropriate for a gallstone diet. It is low in fat, high in fiber, and does not contain any of the ingredients that should be limited or avoided on a gallstone diet. Portobello mushrooms are rich in vitamins and minerals, while spinach and mushrooms contribute extra nutrients and fiber. The use of olive oil and Parmesan cheese is small, resulting in a low-fat level.

Tip: For a vegan variety, you can omit the Parmesan cheese or replace it with a plant-based cheese option.

7. Chickpea Curry (Modified) Low Fat

This modified low-fat Chickpea Curry recipe is a delicious and satisfying option for those following a gallstone-friendly diet. It is rich in taste, fiber, and protein while avoiding high-fat ingredients that can trigger gallbladder discomfort. This hearty and healthy meal that is great for a warm and comforting meal.

INGREDIENTS:

- 1 tablespoon olive oil
- 1 onion, chopped
- 2 cloves garlic, minced
- 1 tablespoon curry powder
- 1 teaspoon ground cumin
- 1/2 teaspoon ground turmeric
- 1/4 teaspoon cayenne pepper (optional)
- 1 (14.5-ounce) can have diced tomatoes, undrained
- 1 (15-ounce) can chickpeas, drained and rinsed
- 1 cup low-sodium vegetable broth
- 1/2 cup chopped cilantro
- Salt and pepper to taste
- Cooked brown rice or quinoa for serving

COOKING INSTRUCTIONS:

1. Heat the olive oil in a large pot or Dutch oven over medium heat. Add the onion and cook until softened about 5 minutes.

2. Add the garlic, curry powder, cumin, turmeric, and cayenne pepper (if using) and cook for 1 minute more, stirring constantly.

3. Add the diced tomatoes, chickpeas, and vegetable broth to the pot. Bring to a boil, then reduce heat and cook for 15-20 minutes, or until the sauce has thickened.

4. Stir in the cilantro and season with salt and pepper to taste.

5. Serve hot cooked brown rice or quinoa.

COOKING TECHNIQUES:

- Onions and spices are sautéed in olive oil to help the taste.

- The curry is simmered to thicken the sauce and meld the taste.

- Calories: 300-350 kcal

- Protein: 15-20 g

- Fat: 5-8 g

- Carbohydrates: 40-45 g

- Fiber: 10-12 g

Serving Portion: This recipe makes 4-6 servings.

Cooking Time: 30-35 minutes

Prep Time: 15 minutes

DIET RECIPE NOTE:

This adapted Chickpea Curry dish is suitable for a gallstone diet. It omits high-fat products like coconut milk and heavy cream, which are commonly used in conventional curry preparations. The combination of lean protein (chickpeas), high-fiber veggies (onion), and whole grains (brown rice or quinoa) results in a nutritious and enjoyable dinner that will not worsen gallbladder symptoms.

Tips:

- For more vegetables, you can add chopped carrots, potatoes, or spinach to the curry.

- Adjust the amount of cayenne pepper to suit your spice liking.

- Leftovers can be stored in the refrigerator for up to 3 days.

8. Vegetable Frittata

This Vegetable Frittata recipe is a delicious and nutritious option for a gallstone-friendly diet. It's rich in fiber-rich vegetables, which can help regulate digestion and promote gallbladder health. Additionally, it's a good source of protein from eggs, and it avoids the use of high-fat ingredients like cheese and cream, which can trigger gallbladder discomfort.

INGREDIENTS:

- 6 large eggs
- 1/4 cup milk (low-fat or plant-based)
- 1 tablespoon olive oil
- 1/2 cup chopped onion
- 1/2 cup chopped bell pepper (any color)
- 1/2 cup chopped broccoli florets
- 1/4 cup chopped mushrooms
- Salt and pepper to taste

COOKING INSTRUCTIONS:

1. Heat oven to 350°F (175°C).

2. In a bowl, mix the eggs and milk. Season with salt and pepper.

3. Heat the olive oil in an oven-safe pan over medium heat. Add the onion and bell pepper and cook until softened about 5 minutes.

4. Add the broccoli and mushrooms and cook for an additional 3-5 minutes, or until soft-crisp.

5. Pour the egg mixture over the vegetables in the pan.

6. Transfer the pan to the heated oven and bake for 15-20 minutes, or until the frittata is set and lightly browned.

7. Let the frittata cool slightly before cutting and serving.

COOKING TECHNIQUES:

- Eggs and milk are mixed to create a smooth mixture.
- Vegetables are sautéed in olive oil to soften and help the taste.

- The frittata is baked in the oven until set and golden brown.

NUTRITIONAL VALUES PER SERVING (APPROXIMATE):

- Calories: 150-200 kcal

- Protein: 10-12 g

- Fat: 8-10 g

- Carbohydrates: 5-8 g

- Fiber: 2-3 g

Serving Portion: This recipe makes 4 servings.

Cooking Time: 20-25 minutes

Prep Time: 10 minutes

Diet Recipe Note:

This Vegetable Frittata recipe is appropriate for a gallstone diet because it avoids all of the foods to limit or avoid on this diet. It is low in fat, high in protein and fiber, and contains no added sugar. The vegetables provide essential nutrients and fiber, which can help regulate digestion and promote gallbladder health.

Tip: Is good to select this recipe by using your favorite vegetables. You can also add herbs and spices like basil, oregano, or paprika for more taste.

_____

_____

_____

_____

_____

9. Zucchini Noodles with Avocado Pesto

This Zucchini Noodles with Avocado Pesto recipe is a light, refreshing, and nutritious meal perfect for a gallstone-friendly diet. Zucchini noodles, also known as *"zoodles,"* *are a low-calorie,* low-carb option to local pasta, making them an excellent choice for individuals managing gallbladder health. The avocado pesto provides healthy fats, fiber, and flavor without the need for cheese or heavy cream, which can trigger gallbladder discomfort.

INGREDIENTS:

- 2-3 medium zucchinis
- 1 ripe avocado
- 1/2 cup fresh basil leaves
- 1/4 cup chopped walnuts or pine nuts
- 2 cloves garlic
- 2 tablespoons lemon juice
- 1/4 cup extra-virgin olive oil
- Salt and pepper to taste

COOKING INSTRUCTIONS:

1. Use a spiralizer or vegetable peeler to create zucchini noodles. Set aside.

2. In a food processor or blender, combine the avocado, basil, walnuts (or pine nuts), garlic, lemon juice, olive oil, salt, and pepper. Blend until smooth and creamy.

3. If the pesto is too thick, add a tablespoon of water at a time until the desired thickness is reached.

4. In a large pan, heat a small amount of olive oil over medium heat. Add the zucchini noodles and cook for 2-3 minutes, or until soft-crisp.

5. Toss the zoodles with the avocado pesto and serve immediately.

COOKING TECHNIQUES:

- Zucchinis are spiralized to create noodle-like strands.
- Pesto ingredients are blended until smooth and creamy.

- Zoodles are lightly sautéed in olive oil.

- Calories: 250-300 kcal

- Protein: 5-7 g

- Fat: 20-25 g (mostly healthy unsaturated fats from avocado and nuts)

- Carbohydrates: 10-15 g

- Fiber: 5-7 g

Serving Portion: This recipe makes 2-3 servings.

Cooking Time: 15 minutes

Prep Time: 10 minutes

DIET RECIPE NOTE:

This Zucchini Noodles with Avocado Pesto dish is suitable for a gallstone diet. It is low in saturated fat, high in fiber, and does not contain any of the ingredients that should be limited or avoided on a gallstone diet. Avocado pesto gives beneficial fats and tastes without the need for cheese or heavy cream.

Tip: For more protein, you can add grilled chicken or shrimp to the meal.

_____

_____

_____

_____

_____

10. Black Bean Soup

This Black Bean Soup recipe is a hearty, delicious, and nutritious option for those following a gallstone-friendly diet. Black beans are a great source of fiber, protein, and essential nutrients, promoting healthy digestion and supporting gallbladder function. This soup is low in fat and cholesterol and can be easily adapted to those liking and dietary needs.

INGREDIENTS:

- 1 tablespoon olive oil
- 1 onion, chopped
- 2 cloves garlic, minced
- 1 red bell pepper, chopped
- 1 teaspoon ground cumin
- 1/2 teaspoon chili powder
- 1/4 teaspoon cayenne pepper (optional)
- 4 cups vegetable broth
- 2 cans (15 ounces each) black beans, drained and rinsed
- 1/4 cup chopped fresh cilantro
- Salt and pepper to taste
- Optional toppings: chopped avocado, diced tomatoes, a dollop of plain Greek yogurt

COOKING INSTRUCTIONS:

1. Heat olive oil in a large pot over medium heat. Add onion and cook until softened about 5 minutes.

2. Add garlic, bell pepper, cumin, chili powder, and cayenne pepper (if using) and cook for another minute.

3. Pour in the vegetable broth and add the black beans. Bring to a boil, then reduce heat and cook for 15 minutes.

4. Use an immersion blender or transfer half the soup to a blender and puree until smooth. Return to the pot.

5. Stir in cilantro and season with salt and pepper to taste.

6. Serve warm with desired toppings.

- Onion, garlic, and bell pepper are sautéed in olive oil to help the taste.

- Soup is cooked to meld flavors and the beans.

- Part of the soup is pureed to create a creamy texture.

NUTRITIONAL VALUES PER SERVING (APPROXIMATE):

- Calories: 250-300 kcal | Protein: 15-20 g | Fat: 5-8 g | Carbohydrates: 35-40 g | Fiber: 15-20 g

Serving Portion: This recipe makes about 6 servings.

Cooking Time: 30 minutes

Prep Time: 15 minutes

DIET RECIPE NOTE:

This Black Bean Soup is ideal for a gallstone diet since it is strong in fiber and free of animal fats and processed carbohydrates. If you use low-sodium broth, it will be low in sodium as well. Adjust the spice level or add additional veggies to suit your tastes and dietary demands.

Tip: For more flavor, consider adding a bay leaf during cooking and removing it before serving.

Self-Reflection Questions:

1. What are my current dietary habits regarding vegetarian or vegan meals, and how can I adapt them to be more gallstone-friendly?

_____

_____

_____

_____

2. Am I willing to explore new vegetarian or vegan recipes to support my gallbladder health?

_____

_____

_____

3. What are my primary concerns or challenges in transitioning to a more plant-based diet, and how can I address them?

_____

_____

_____

_____

_____

4. How can I ensure I'm getting adequate protein and nutrients on a vegetarian or vegan gallstone-friendly diet?

_____

_____

_____

_____

_____

5. What resources (cookbooks, online communities, etc.) can I utilize to support my journey towards a plant-based lifestyle that benefits my gallbladder?

_____

_____

_____

_____

CHAPTER 9:

GALLBLADDER DIET SMOOTHIES

1. Juice - Cucumber Mint Cooler

This Cucumber Mint Cooler is a refreshing and hydrating beverage great for a gallstone-friendly diet. It's made with simple, natural ingredients that are easy to digest and won't irritate your gallbladder. Cucumbers are hydrating and low in calories, while mint adds a refreshing taste and can aid digestion. This cooler is a delicious way to stay hydrated and support your gallbladder health.

INGREDIENTS:

- 1 cucumber, peeled and chopped
- 1/2 cup fresh mint leaves
- 1 lime, juiced
- 1 cup water
- Ice cubes (optional)

PREPARATION INSTRUCTIONS:

1. Combine all ingredients in a blender and blend until smooth.

2. Strain the mixture through a fine-mesh sieve if desired (this will remove any pulp and create a smoother juice).

3. Add ice cubes if desired and serve immediately.

PREPARATION TECHNIQUES:

- Cucumber and mint leaves are chopped for easier blending.
- All ingredients are blended until smooth.
- Optional step to remove pulp and create a smoother juice.

NUTRITIONAL VALUES PER SERVING (APPROXIMATE):

- Calories: 40-50 kcal
- Protein: 1-2 g

- Fat: 0-1 g

- Carbohydrates: 8-10 g

- Fiber: 1-2 g

Serving Portion: This recipe makes 1-2 servings.

Prep Time: 5 minutes

Tip: For a sweeter drink, add a natural sweetener like honey or agave nectar. However, be mindful of the amount to keep the sugar content low.

2. Strawberry Banana Smoothie

This Strawberry Banana Smoothie recipe is a refreshing and nutritious option for those following a gallstone-friendly diet. It's rich in vitamins, minerals, and fiber from fresh fruits and can be a great way to start your day or enjoy as a healthy snack.

INGREDIENTS:

- 1 cup frozen strawberries
- 1 ripe banana
- 1/2 cup unsweetened almond milk (or other low-fat milk alternative)
- 1/4 cup plain Greek yogurt (optional, for added creaminess and protein)

PREPARATION INSTRUCTIONS:

1. Combine all ingredients in a blender.
2. Blend until smooth and creamy.
3. If the smoothie is too thick, add a splash more almond milk.
4. Pour into a glass and enjoy immediately

PREPARATION TECHNIQUES:

- Wash the strawberries and bananas, then chop them into smaller pieces for easier blending.
- All ingredients are blended until smooth and creamy.

NUTRITIONAL VALUES PER SERVING (APPROXIMATE):

- Calories: 150-200 kcal (depending on ingredients and portion size)
- Protein: 4-6 g (higher if Greek yogurt is added)
- Fat: 1-3 g
- Carbohydrates: 30-35 g
- Fiber: 4-5 g

Serving Portion: This recipe makes one large serving or two smaller servings.

Prep Time: 5 minutes

Variety:

- **Tropical Twist:** Add 1/2 cup of frozen mango or pineapple chunks for a tropical taste.
- **Protein Boost:** Add a scoop of protein powder or a tablespoon of nut butter for added protein.
- **Green Power:** Add a handful of spinach or kale for more nutrients and fiber.

3. Strawberry Oatmeal Smoothie

This Strawberry Oatmeal Smoothie recipe is a nutritious and refreshing option for those following a gallstone-friendly diet. It's rich in fiber from oats and strawberries, providing a satisfying and energy-boosting breakfast or snack. It's also low in fat and cholesterol, making it a safe and delicious choice for supporting gallbladder health.

INGREDIENTS:

- 1 cup unsweetened almond milk (or other low-fat milk option)
- 1/2 cup rolled oats
- 1/2 cup frozen strawberries
- 1/2 ripe banana
- 1 tablespoon chia seeds (optional)
- 1 teaspoon honey or maple syrup (optional, for added sweetness)

PREPARATION INSTRUCTIONS:

1. Combine all ingredients in a blender.
2. Blend until smooth and creamy.
3. If the smoothie is too thick, add a splash more almond milk.
4. Pour into a glass and enjoy immediately.

PREPARATION TECHNIQUES:

- All ingredients are blended until smooth.

NUTRITIONAL VALUES PER SERVING (APPROXIMATE):

- Calories: 200-250 kcal | Protein: 5-7 g | Fat: 3-5 g
- Carbohydrates: 35-40 g | Fiber: 5-7 g

Serving Portion: This recipe makes one large serving.

Prep Time: 5 minutes

Tips:

- Is good to try different fruits and berries based on your preferences and what's in season.
- Add a scoop of protein powder for a more boost if desired.
- If you prefer a sweeter smoothie, add a sprinkle of honey or maple syrup.
- For added creaminess, you can add a spoonful of plain Greek yogurt or a few tablespoons of silken tofu.

4. Peanut Butter Banana Protein Shake

This Peanut Butter Banana Protein Shake is a delicious and nutritious option for a gallstone-friendly breakfast or snack. It's rich in protein, fiber, and healthy fats, making it a satisfying and energizing option that supports gallbladder health.

INGREDIENTS:

- 1 ripe banana, frozen
- 1 tablespoon natural peanut butter (no added sugar or oils)
- 1 scoop of plant-based protein powder (such as pea or hemp protein)
- 1 cup unsweetened almond milk or other non-dairy milk
- 1/2 teaspoon vanilla extract (optional)
- Pinch of cinnamon (optional)
- Ice cubes (optional)

PREPARATION INSTRUCTIONS:

1. Combine all ingredients in a blender.
2. Blend until smooth and creamy.
3. If you want, add a few ice cubes and blend again for a colder, thicker shake.
4. Pour into a glass and enjoy immediately.

PREPARATION TECHNIQUES:

- All ingredients are combined and blended until smooth.

NUTRITIONAL VALUES PER SERVING (APPROXIMATE):

- Calories: 250-350 kcal (depending on protein powder and milk choice)
- Protein: 20-30 g
- Fat: 10-15 g (mostly healthy unsaturated fats from peanut butter)
- Carbohydrates: 20-30 g
- Fiber: 5-8 g

Serving Portion: This recipe makes one large shake or two smaller servings.

Prep Time: 5 minutes

Tip: For a more taste boost, consider adding a handful of spinach or kale to the shake. You won't taste the greens, but they will add valuable nutrients.

5. Blueberry Cheesecake Smoothie

This Blueberry Cheesecake Smoothie is a delicious and nutritious way to satisfy your sweet cravings while adhering to a gallstone-friendly diet. It's rich in antioxidants from blueberries, protein from Greek yogurt, and healthy fats from almonds, making it a balanced and satisfying snack or breakfast option.

INGREDIENTS:

- 1 cup frozen blueberries
- 1/2 cup plain non-fat Greek yogurt
- 1/4 cup unsweetened almond milk
- 1/4 cup raw almonds
- 1/2 teaspoon vanilla extract
- 1/4 teaspoon ground cinnamon
- Pinch of nutmeg
- Optional sweetener: 1-2 teaspoons honey or maple syrup (depending on your preference)

PREPARATION INSTRUCTIONS:

1. Combine all ingredients in a high-powered blender.

2. Blend until smooth and creamy. If the smoothie is too thick, add a splash more almond milk. If you prefer it sweeter, add honey or maple syrup to taste.

3. Pour into a glass and enjoy immediately.

PREPARATION TECHNIQUES:

- The key technique is blending all ingredients until smooth and creamy.

NUTRITIONAL VALUES PER SERVING (APPROXIMATE):

- Calories: 250-300 kcal | Protein: 15-20 g | Fat: 10-15 g | Carbohydrates: 20-25 g | Fiber: 5-7 g

Serving Portion: This recipe makes one large serving or two smaller servings.

Prep Time: 5 minutes

Tips:

- For a thicker smoothie, use frozen Greek yogurt.
- Add a handful of spinach or kale for a more boost of nutrients.
- Try with other berries like strawberries or raspberries.
- If you don't have almond milk, you can use any other type of unsweetened milk.

6. Cottage Cheese Fruit Smoothie

This Cottage Cheese Fruit Smoothie is a creamy, protein-rich, and refreshing snack or breakfast option that aligns greatly with a gallstone-friendly diet. Cottage cheese is a low-fat dairy option that provides vital nutrients like calcium and protein, while fruits contribute fiber and vitamins. This smoothie avoids high-fat dairy and added sugars, making it a safe and satisfying choice for individuals with gallbladder concerns.

INGREDIENTS:

- 1 cup low-fat or non-fat cottage cheese

- 1/2 cup frozen or fresh berries (such as strawberries, blueberries, or raspberries)

- 1/2 banana

- 1/2 cup unsweetened almond milk or other low-fat milk alternative

- 1/4 teaspoon vanilla extract (optional)

- Pinch of cinnamon (optional)

PREPARATION INSTRUCTIONS:

1. Combine all ingredients in a blender.

2. Blend until smooth and creamy.

3. If you want, add a few ice cubes and blend again for a colder and thicker smoothie.

4. Pour into a glass and enjoy immediately.

PREPARATION TECHNIQUES:

- All ingredients are blended until smooth and creamy.

NUTRITIONAL VALUES PER SERVING (APPROXIMATE):

- Calories: 200-250 kcal | Protein: 15-20 g | Fat: 5-8 g | Carbohydrates: 20-25 g | Fiber: 4-6 g

Serving Portion: This recipe makes one large serving or two smaller servings.

Prep Time: 5 minutes

Tips:

- Use frozen fruit for a thicker, colder smoothie.

- Try with different fruits and taste.

- Add a handful of spinach or kale for more nutrients.

- For added protein, consider adding a scoop of protein powder.

- Adjust the amount of milk to achieve your desired thickness.

7. Pineapple Orange Banana Smoothie

This Pineapple Orange Banana Smoothie is a refreshing, nutritious, and gallstone-friendly way to start your day or enjoy a midday snack. Rich in vitamins, minerals, and fiber, this smoothie is both delicious and supportive of gallbladder health. It's naturally sweet and requires no added sugar, making it a great choice for those looking to manage their blood sugar levels as well.

INGREDIENTS:

- 1 cup frozen pineapple chunks

- 1 ripe banana, sliced and frozen

- 1 orange, peeled and segmented

- 1/2 cup unsweetened almond milk or coconut milk

- 1/4 cup plain non-fat Greek yogurt (optional, for extra protein)

- 1/2 cup ice cubes (optional, for a thicker smoothie)

PREPARATION INSTRUCTIONS:

1. Place all ingredients in a blender.

2. Blend on high speed until smooth and creamy.

3. If the smoothie is too thick, add a little more almond milk or coconut milk until the desired thickness is reached.

4. Pour into a glass and enjoy immediately.

PREPARATION TECHNIQUES:

- Freezing the fruit beforehand helps create a thicker, icier smoothie.

- All ingredients are blended until smooth and creamy.

NUTRITIONAL VALUES PER SERVING (APPROXIMATE):

- Calories: 150-200 kcal | Protein: 4-5 g (with Greek yogurt) | Fat: 2-3 g | Carbohydrates: 30-35 g | Fiber: 4-5 g

Serving Portion: This recipe makes one large serving or two smaller servings.

Prep Time: 5-10 minutes

Tips:

- Feel free to adjust the amount of liquid to achieve your desired thickness.

- For a tropical twist, add a handful of spinach or kale to the smoothie.

- If you don't have frozen fruit, you can use fresh fruit and add a few ice cubes.

8. Blueberry Tofu Smoothie

This Blueberry Tofu Smoothie recipe is a creamy, nutritious, and delicious option for those following a gallstone-friendly diet. Tofu is a low-fat, high-protein plant-based protein source, while blueberries are rich in antioxidants and fiber, both of which are beneficial for gallbladder health. This smoothie is a great way to start your day or enjoy as a refreshing snack.

INGREDIENTS:

- 1/2 cup silken tofu
- 1 cup frozen blueberries
- 1/2 ripe banana
- 1/2 cup unsweetened almond milk or soy milk
- 1 tablespoon chia seeds (optional)
- 1/2 teaspoon vanilla extract (optional)

PREPARATION INSTRUCTIONS:

1. Combine all ingredients in a blender.
2. Blend until smooth and creamy.
3. If the smoothie is too thick, add a splash of more milk until the desired thickness is reached.
4. Pour into a glass and enjoy immediately.

PREPARATION TECHNIQUES:

- All ingredients are blended until smooth and creamy.

NUTRITIONAL VALUES PER SERVING (APPROXIMATE):

- Calories: 200-250 kcal
- Protein: 10-12 g
- Fat: 5-8 g
- Carbohydrates: 25-30 g
- Fiber: 4-6 g

Serving Portion: This recipe makes one serving.

Prep Time: 5 minutes

Tip: To increase the fiber content of this smoothie, you can add a handful of spinach or kale. For more sweetness, you can add a sprinkle of honey or maple syrup, but use it sparingly.

CHAPTER 10:
30-DAY GALLSTONE DIET RECOVERY MEAL PLAN

Day 1:

- **Breakfast:** Greek Yogurt Parfait

- **Lunch:** Quinoa Stuffed Bell Peppers

- **Dinner:** Baked Chicken Breast with Roasted Sweet Potatoes and Green Beans

- **Snack:** Chia Pudding with Mango Puree

Day 2:

- **Breakfast:** Oatmeal with Almond Milk and Berries

- **Lunch:** Veggie Stir-Fry with Brown Rice

- **Dinner:** Grilled Tilapia with Lemon Herb Quinoa

- **Snack:** Pineapple and Cottage Cheese

Day 3:

- **Breakfast:** Scrambled Tofu with Vegetables

- **Lunch:** Grilled Chicken Salad with Mixed Greens and Balsamic Vinaigrette

- **Dinner:** Vegan Chili with Sweet Potato and Black Beans

- **Snack:** Baked Apples with Oats and Raisins

Day 4:

- **Breakfast:** Gallstone-Friendly Sweet Potato Hash

- **Lunch:** Quinoa Salad with Cucumber, Tomato, and Lemon Dressing

- **Dinner:** Baked Salmon with Steamed Broccoli

- **Snack:** Beans & Cauliflower Hummus

Day 5:

- **Breakfast:** Green Smoothie Bowl

- **Lunch:** Wraps with Lettuce and Tuna Salad

- **Dinner:** Zucchini Noodles with Tomato Basil Sauce

- **Snack:** Strawberry Sorbet

Day 6:

- **Breakfast:** Vegetable Omelet

- **Lunch:** Lentil Soup

- **Dinner:** Cod with a Citrus and Herb Crust

- **Snack:** Baked Apples with Cinnamon

Day 7:

- **Breakfast:** Sautéed Greens with Poached Egg

- **Lunch:** Grilled Chicken Salad

- **Dinner:** Turkey Meatballs with Spaghetti Squash

- **Snack:** Raspberry and Lemon Gelatin

Day 8:

- **Breakfast:** Avocado Toast with Smoked Salmon

- **Lunch:** Pumpkin Soup with Toasted Whole Grain Bread

- **Dinner:** Veggie Lasagna with Eggplant and Zucchini

- **Snack:** Pear and Almond Crumble

Day 9:

- **Breakfast:** Spinach and Mushroom Frittata

- **Lunch:** Italian Sausage and Peppers

- **Dinner:** Moroccan Chicken with Couscous

- **Snack:** Black Bean Dip

Day 10:

- **Breakfast:** Chia Seed Pudding

- **Lunch:** Chicken and Vegetable Sticks

- **Dinner:** Sautéed Shrimp with Garlic and Herbs over Zoodles

- **Snack:** Apricot and Yogurt Parfait

Day 11:

- **Breakfast:** Quinoa Breakfast Bowl

- **Lunch:** Salmon and Quinoa Bowl

- **Dinner:** Stuffed Bell Peppers with Ground Turkey and Quinoa

- **Snack:** Corn & Beans Relish

Day 12:

- **Breakfast:** Smashed Chickpea Salad Wrap

- **Lunch:** Greek Salad with Grilled Shrimp

- **Dinner:** Butternut Squash Risotto

- **Snack:** Berries Gazpacho

Day 13:

- **Breakfast:** Sweet Potato Hash Browns

- **Lunch:** Vegetable Quinoa Wrap

- **Dinner:** Lentil Stew with Kale and Potatoes

- **Snack:** Baked Peaches with Honey and Greek Yogurt

Day 14:

- **Breakfast:** Quinoa Breakfast Burrito

- **Lunch:** Turkey Lettuce Wraps

- **Dinner:** Eggplant Parmesan with Low-Fat Mozzarella

- **Snack:** Chickpeas & Carrot Hummus

Day 15:

- **Breakfast:** Salmon and Vegetable Quiche

- **Lunch:** Quinoa and Vegetable Stir-Fry

- **Dinner:** Baked Chicken Breast with Roasted Sweet Potatoes and Green Beans

- **Snack:** Chia Pudding with Mango Puree

Day 16:

- **Breakfast:** Greek Yogurt Parfait
- **Lunch:** Veggie Stir-Fry with Brown Rice
- **Dinner:** Cod with a Citrus and Herb Crust
- **Snack:** Baked Apples with Oats and Raisins

Day 17:

- **Breakfast:** Oatmeal with Almond Milk and Berries
- **Lunch:** Grilled Chicken Salad
- **Dinner:** Turkey Meatballs with Spaghetti Squash
- **Snack:** Pineapple and Cottage Cheese

Day 18:

- **Breakfast:** Scrambled Tofu with Vegetables
- **Lunch:** Pumpkin Soup with Toasted Whole Grain Bread
- **Dinner:** Veggie Lasagna with Eggplant and Zucchini
- **Snack:** Beans & Cauliflower Hummus

Day 19:

- **Breakfast:** Gallstone-Friendly Sweet Potato Hash
- **Lunch:** Italian Sausage and Peppers
- **Dinner:** Moroccan Chicken with Couscous

- **Snack:** Strawberry Sorbet

Day 20:

- **Breakfast:** Green Smoothie Bowl
- **Lunch:** Chicken and Vegetable Sticks
- **Dinner:** Sautéed Shrimp with Garlic and Herbs over Zoodles
- **Snack:** Baked Apples with Cinnamon

Day 21:

- **Breakfast:** Vegetable Omelet
- **Lunch:** Quinoa Salad with Cucumber, Tomato, and Lemon Dressing
- **Dinner:** Baked Salmon with Steamed Broccoli
- **Snack:** Raspberry and Lemon Gelatin

Day 22:

- **Breakfast:** Sautéed Greens with Poached Egg
- **Lunch:** Wraps with Lettuce and Tuna Salad
- **Dinner:** Vegan Chili with Sweet Potato and Black Beans
- **Snack:** Pear and Almond Crumble

Day 23:

- **Breakfast:** Avocado Toast with Smoked Salmon
- **Lunch:** Lentil Soup
- **Dinner:** Stuffed Bell Peppers with Ground Turkey and Quinoa
- **Snack:** Black Bean Dip

Day 24:

- **Breakfast:** Spinach and Mushroom Frittata

- **Lunch:** Greek Salad with Grilled Shrimp

- **Dinner:** Butternut Squash Risotto

- **Snack:** Apricot and Yogurt Parfait

Day 25:

- **Breakfast:** Chia Seed Pudding

- **Lunch:** Vegetable Quinoa Wrap

- **Dinner:** Lentil Stew with Kale and Potatoes

- **Snack:** Corn & Beans Relish

Day 26:

- **Breakfast:** Quinoa Breakfast Bowl

- **Lunch:** Salmon and Quinoa Bowl

- **Dinner:** Eggplant Parmesan with Low-Fat Mozzarella

- **Snack:** Berries Gazpacho

Day 27:

- **Breakfast:** Smashed Chickpea Salad Wrap

- **Lunch:** Turkey Lettuce Wraps

- **Dinner:** Baked Chicken Breast with Roasted Sweet Potatoes and Green Beans

- **Snack:** Chickpeas & Carrot Hummus

Day 28:

- **Breakfast:** Sweet Potato Hash Browns

- **Lunch:** Quinoa and Vegetable Stir-Fry

- **Dinner:** Grilled Tilapia with Lemon Herb Quinoa

- **Snack:** Chia Pudding with Mango Puree

Day 29:

- **Breakfast:** Quinoa Breakfast Burrito

- **Lunch:** Pumpkin Soup with Toasted Whole Grain Bread

- **Dinner:** Cod with a Citrus and Herb Crust

- **Snack:** Pineapple and Cottage Cheese

Day 30:

- **Breakfast:** Salmon and Vegetable Quiche

- **Lunch:** Grilled Chicken Salad with Mixed Greens and Balsamic Vinaigrette

- **Dinner:** Turkey Meatballs with Spaghetti Squash

- **Snack:** Baked Peaches with Honey and Greek Yogurt

CHAPTER 11:
LIFESTYLE TIPS FOR A HEALTHY GALLBLADDER

Stress Management Techniques

In the intricate connection between mind and body, stress can disrupt the harmony within us. While we often associate stress with heart problems or high blood pressure, it's easy to overlook its impact on our gallbladder. Yet, research shows that stress can indeed influence this small but vital organ.

Imagine stress as a ripple effect, beginning in your mind and extending throughout your body. When stress hits, your body releases cortisol and adrenaline, which trigger physiological changes like a faster heart rate, higher blood pressure, and altered digestion. Your gallbladder, responsible for storing and releasing bile for digestion, feels the impact of these changes. Stress can disrupt the normal flow of bile, potentially leading to gallstones or painful attacks.

One way stress affects gallbladder health is by raising cholesterol levels. Studies reveal that chronic stress can increase cholesterol production, a key ingredient in gallstone formation. Additionally, stress hinders the body's ability to break down and eliminate cholesterol, further increasing the risk.

Stress also affects the muscles in your digestive system, including your gallbladder. Normally, these muscles contract and relax to move bile, but chronic stress can make them tense and uncoordinated, slowing bile flow and raising the risk of gallstones.

Moreover, stress takes a toll on your overall well-being, making it harder for your body to heal and function properly. When you're constantly stressed, your immune system weakens, inflammation rises, and digestion suffers. This creates an unfavorable environment for your gallbladder, potentially worsening existing conditions or causing new ones.

But don't lose hope. You have the power to manage stress. Just as stress can harm your gallbladder, relaxation and stress-management techniques can have a positive impact. By accepting these practices, you can create a calmer internal environment, reduce inflammation, and support a healthy gallbladder.

Meditation is a powerful tool for stress reduction. It involves focusing on the present moment and releasing worries. Regular meditation can lower cortisol levels, reduce inflammation, and boost well-being. Even a few minutes each day can make a difference.

Deep breathing is another effective technique. When stressed, your breathing becomes shallow. By consciously slowing down and deepening your breath, you activate your body's relaxation response, lowering your heart rate and calming your nervous system. Deep breathing can be done anywhere, anytime.

Yoga, with its blend of physical postures, breathing exercises, and mindfulness, is also excellent for stress reduction. Yoga stretches release muscle tension, while the focus on breath and the present moment promotes relaxation. Regular yoga practice has been shown to improve mood, reduce anxiety, and enhance overall well-being.

Sleep, often neglected in our busy lives, is crucial for stress management and overall health. Sleep is when your body repairs and rejuvenates itself. Lack of sleep disrupts hormones, increases inflammation, and weakens the immune system. Aim for 7-8 hours of quality sleep each night for optimal health.

Besides these techniques, find healthy ways to relax and unwind. Spend time in nature, listen to calming music, take warm baths, or pursue hobbies you enjoy. The key is to find activities that disconnect you from stressors and recharge you.

Managing stress is an ongoing process. It's about incorporating healthy habits into your routine and discovering what works for you. By prioritizing relaxation and stress reduction, you not only support your gallbladder health but also enhance your overall quality of life.

Exercising for Gallbladder Health

Regular exercise is a cornerstone of gallbladder health. It can help stimulate bile flow, prevent stagnation, and reduce the risk of gallstone formation. Additionally, maintaining a healthy weight through exercise can reduce the likelihood of developing gallstones.

Activities:

- **Walking:** Start with 15–20-minute walks and gradually increase the duration and pace.

Aim for at least 30 minutes of brisk walking most days of the week.

- **Swimming:** The buoyancy of water makes swimming a gentle yet effective exercise for overall fitness and gallbladder health.

  Aim for 20–30-minute sessions, 2-3 times a week.

- **Cycling:** Whether on a stationary bike or outdoors, cycling is a great way to get your heart rate up.

  Start with shorter rides (15-20 minutes) and gradually increase the duration as you build endurance.

- **Yoga:** Gentle yoga poses like twists and forward folds can help stimulate the gallbladder and improve digestion.

  Focus on proper form and avoid any poses that cause discomfort.

- **Pilates:** Pilates strengthens your core muscles, which can aid in digestion and promote overall well-being. Look for beginner classes or online tutorials to get started.

Precautions and Tips:

- **Listen to Your Body:** Pay attention to how your body feels during and after exercise. Stop if you experience pain or discomfort.

- **Start Slowly:** If you're new to exercise, begin with shorter durations and lower intensity. Gradually increase the duration and intensity as your fitness level improves.

- **Stay Hydrated:** Drink plenty of water before, during, and after exercise to stay hydrated and support healthy bile flow.

- **Warm-Up and Cool Down:** Always start your workout with a gentle warm-up (like light cardio or stretching) and end with a cool-down to prevent injury.

Important Considerations:

- **High-Impact Activities:** High-impact exercises like running or jumping can put stress on your abdomen and may trigger gallbladder pain. Option for low-impact activities instead.

- **Intense Exercise:** Avoid overexerting yourself, especially if you're new to exercise or have a history of gallbladder issues. Listen to your body and take breaks when needed.

- **Post-Meal Exercise:** It's generally recommended to wait at least an hour after eating before exercising to allow your body to digest food properly.

_____

_____

_____

_____

_____

_____

_____

_____

_____

CHAPTER 12:
GALLBLADDER-FRIENDLY EXERCISE PLAN FOR BEGINNERS

Week 1:

- **Day 1:** 20-minute brisk walk

- **Day 2:** Gentle yoga or Pilates (30 minutes)

- **Day 3:** Rest or light stretching

- **Day 4:** 20-minute swim or water aerobics

- **Day 5:** 30-minute walk

- **Day 6:** Yoga or Pilates (30 minutes)

- **Day 7:** Rest or active recovery (e.g., stretching, foam rolling)

Week 2:

- **Day 8:** 25-minute brisk walk

- **Day 9:** Swimming or water aerobics (30 minutes)

- **Day 10:** Rest or light stretching

- **Day 11:** 25-minute bike ride (stationary or outdoor)

- **Day 12:** Yoga or Pilates (30 minutes)

- **Day 13:** 30-minute walk

- **Day 14:** Rest or active recovery

Important Notes:

- **Listen to your body:** If you experience any pain or discomfort, stop the activity and rest.

- **Stay hydrated:** Drink plenty of water before, during, and after exercise.

- **Warm-up and cool-down:** Always start with a 5–10-minute warm-up and end with a cool-down to prevent injury.

- **Progression:** Gradually increase the duration or intensity of your workouts as you get stronger.

- **Variety:** Mix up your activities to avoid boredom and work different muscle groups.

CONCLUSION

"Let food be thy medicine and medicine be thy food."

Hippocrates

Remember, a gallstone diagnosis isn't a life sentence to bland meals. It's an opportunity to start on a delicious journey, discovering new ingredients, flavors, and cooking techniques that nourish your body and delight your taste buds. The recipes in this book are more than just a collection of dishes; they're a state of belief or give some kind of direction to the fact that eating for gallbladder health can be both enjoyable and satisfying.

We've learned that the foundation of a gallstone-friendly diet is simple yet powerful: prioritize low-fat, high-fiber, and balanced meals. By incorporating plenty of fruits, vegetables, whole grains, lean proteins, and healthy fats into your daily routine, you can reduce your risk of gallstone formation, manage symptoms, and promote overall digestive well-being.

But it's not just about what you eat; it's also about how you prepare your food. We've explored various cooking methods, such as baking, grilling, steaming, and sautéing, that allow you to create flavorful dishes without relying on unhealthy fats or frying. We've

also emphasized the importance of using fresh, whole ingredients and minimizing processed foods, added sugars, and refined grains.

Beyond the kitchen, we've gone into the significance of exercise in maintaining gallbladder health. Regular physical activity, such as walking, swimming, or yoga, can help stimulate bile flow, reduce cholesterol levels, and promote weight management – all of which are crucial for preventing gallstones.

We've also touched upon the importance of stress management and mindful eating. Stress can trigger gallbladder contractions and exacerbate symptoms, while mindful eating can help you tune into your body's hunger and fullness cues, preventing overeating and promoting healthy digestion. They can help you personalize your diet and exercise plan to meet your individual needs and address any specific concerns you may have.

Remember, this cookbook is just the beginning of your journey toward improved gallbladder health. It's a tool to empower you, to give you the knowledge and inspiration you need to make informed choices about your diet and lifestyle. By accepting the principles outlined in this book, you can take control of your health, reduce your risk of gallstone complications, and enjoy a life filled with vitality and delicious food.

As you continue on this path, remember that you're not alone. Millions of people worldwide are living with gallstones, and many have successfully managed their condition through dietary and lifestyle changes. There are also numerous online communities and support groups where you can connect with others who share your journey.

So, keep exploring, keep experimenting, and keep discovering the joy of eating for health. With a little creativity and a willingness to embrace change, you can transform your diet into a powerful tool for healing and well-being. Your gallbladder will thank you, and you'll be rewarded with a life filled with flavor, energy, and vitality.

Let this cookbook be your constant companion on this journey. Refer to it often for inspiration, guidance, and delicious recipes that will nourish your body and delight your soul. Remember, the power to transform your health is in your hands – and on your plate.

Dear Reader,

Thank you for joining me on this journey to better gallbladder health with the *Gallstone Diet Cookbook for Newly Diagnosed*. It's my sincere hope that the recipes and information within these pages have empowered you to take charge of your health and well-being through delicious, nourishing food.

As a special thank you for your support, I've prepared a small gift: [**Audio Affirmation** and a **Meal Planner Journal in Paperback and Hardcover**]. You can access it by [buying the paperback or hardcover and using a unique **QR Code** included in the book to access the affirmation].

Remember, you are not alone in this journey. May this cookbook be your companion as you discover the joy of eating for health and happiness.

With warmest wishes,

Mary J. Barnes RDN

How to Access the Affirmation Audio

SCAM THIS TO ACCESS YOUR GIFT

Meal Planner Journal And Exercise Observations

Meal Planner Journal And Exercise Observations

Meal Planner Journal And Exercise Observations

Meal Planner Journal And Exercise Observations

Meal Planner Journal And Exercise Observations

Meal Planner Journal And Exercise Observations

Meal Planner Journal And Exercise Observations

Meal Planner Journal And Exercise Observations

Meal Planner Journal And Exercise Observations

Meal Planner Journal And Exercise Observations

Meal Planner Journal And Exercise Observations

Meal Planner Journal And Exercise Observations

Meal Planner Journal And Exercise Observations

Meal Planner Journal And Exercise Observations

Meal Planner Journal And Exercise Observations

Meal Planner Journal And Exercise Observations

Meal Planner Journal And Exercise Observations

Meal Planner Journal And Exercise Observations

Made in the USA
Las Vegas, NV
30 November 2024

12998784R00111